Early Families

— of —

Frederick County

Maryland

— and —

Adams County

Pennsylvania

Steve Gilland

HERITAGE BOOKS
2006

HERITAGE BOOKS

AN IMPRINT OF HERITAGE BOOKS, INC.

Books, CDs, and more—Worldwide

For our listing of thousands of titles see our website
at
www.HeritageBooks.com

Published 2006 by
HERITAGE BOOKS, INC.
Publishing Division
65 East Main Street
Westminster, Maryland 21157-5026

Other books by the author:

Early Families of Frederick County, Maryland, and South Central Pennsylvania
Frederick County Backgrounds

International Standard Book Number: 978-1-58549-423-2

Dedicated to my grandparents
John and Nellie Cline Gilland.

TABLE OF CONTENTS

INTRODUCTION

"There is a regard for ancestry which
nourishes only a weak pride, but there is
also a moral and philosophical respect for
our ancestry which elevates the character
and improves the heart. Next to the sense
of religious duty and moral feeling, I
hardly know what should bear stronger
obligation on a liberal and enlightened
mind than a consciousness of alliance with
the excellance which has departed."
- Daniel Webster.

Frederick County was formed in 1748 from Baltimore
and Prince George's Counties. At that time Frederick
County comprised the entire western part of the state
of Maryland. As the population grew Frederick County
was divided and in 1776 Montgomery and Washington
Counties were formed. Later Allegany, Carroll, and
Garrett Counties were formed from what was originally
Frederick County.

This is a study of some of the founding father's
and mother's footsteps that have been traced throughout
Maryland, as well as New York, New Jersey, Delaware,
and Pennsylvania. Research has revealed that these
these early ancestors had a role in our country's
history. They were among the early settlers and
pioneers, the founding members of churches, towns,
and settlements, soldiers of the great wars of freedom
and independence, and revolutionaries of religious
freedom and liberty of conscience. Through these early
ancestors their descendants share a very proud and
prolific heritage.

This is a compilation of the data that I have at this
time, and have written for you, to create interest, and
partly in hope that you will correct any errors or
supply additional information to form a more complete
and accurate record.
- Steve Gilland, Gettysburg, Pennsylvania, 1996.

LINEAGE CHART
MATHIAS(1) AMBROSE 1696-1784, m CATHERINE SPONGH 1711-1807.
JOHN 'PHILIP'(2) AMBROSE 1734-1776, m EVA CATHERINE.
HENRY(3) AMBROSE 1763-1845, m SOPHIA WEAVER 1769-1841.
ELIZABETH(4) AMBROSE 1791-1856, m PHILIP CLINE 1786-1874.

MATHIAS(1) AMBROSE 1696-1784.
Mathias was born about 1696 in Germany. In 1732 he emigrated
to America arriving at the port of Philadelphia, Pennsylvania.
According to the ship passenger list he was 37 years old and was
on board the ship Pleasant. In 1733 he was married to 21 year
old Catherine Spongh. Catherine was born in Germany on December
15, 1711, the daughter of Adam Spongh. They settled at Muddy
Creek, in the Conestoga area of Lancaster County, Pennsylvania.
Here their son John Philip was born in 1734 and was baptized by
the Rev. John Casper Stover.
    By 1739, Mathias and his family had moved to Frederick County,
Maryland. He is listed among the early European settlers of the
Upper Monocacy Valley, in the Backlands, north of present day
Thurmont. In 1743 he received communion and was naturalized at
the Monocacy Lutheran Church.
    Mathias was a miller and a farmer and his mill, known as
Ambrose Mill, the forerunner of Thurmont, was located on Owen's
Creek. Ambrose Mill was a landmark and appeared on the land
records from 1743 to 1759. In 1760 Mathias and his son Jacob
and Jacob Mathias were the trustees for Jacob's, now Apple's
Church. By 1763 Mathias had aquired over 700 acres in the
Thurmont - Monocacy area.
    Mathias died in 1784 and was interred at Apple's Church Ceme-
tery. His will was written October 19, 1782 and probated October 16, 1784. He gave three pounds sterling to Jacob's Church
and the remainder of his estate to his daughter Catherine and
her husband John Weller, stating that the rest of his children
had received their share.
    Erected in Apple's Cemetery is a weathered tombstone with the
following German inscription:- Mathys Ambroj / gebd 10 Feb /
1696 / Verfch d 10 Aug / 1784 / Alt 87 Jahr 6 M / Wen: 3 Tag.
Mathias Ambrose / born 10 Feb / 1696 / Died 10 Aug / 1784 /
Aged 87 Years 6 Months / and 3 Days.
    Mathias and Catherine were the parents of 7 children:-
1. JOHN 'PHILIP' AMBROSE 1734-1776. Philip was born in 1734
   at Muddy Creek, Lancaster County, Pennsylvania. He was
   married to EVA CATHERINE and resided in Frederick County,
   Maryland.
2. Henry Ambrose was born October 13, 1736, and was baptised
   as Augustus Heinrick by the Rev. Stover at Muddy Creek on
   January 6, 1737. In 1759 he received 160 acres, a part of
   the tract Arnold's Chance, from his father Mathias Ambrose.

3. Mathias Ambrose Jr. was born March 20, 1739, and was baptized
   by the Rev. Stover, at Monocacy on June 17, 1739. In 1759 he
   received 170 acres, a part of the tract Arnold's Chance, from
   his father Mathias Ambrose.
4. Johann Frederick Ambrose was baptized in 1741.
5. Maria Barbara Ambrose was born January 24, 1743 and baptized
   June 13, 1743 by the Rev. Chandler. In 1759 she received
   170 acres, a part of Arnold's Chance, from her father Mathias
   Ambrose.
6. Catherine Salome Ambrose was married to John Weller Sr. In
   1796, Catherine and some of her children moved to Nelson
   County, Kentucky.
7. Jacob Ambrose received the tract Gap, 100 acres, north of
   Thurmont, from his parents, Mathias and Catherine Ambrose.

JOHN 'PHILIP'(2) AMBROSE 1734-1776.

John Philip was born in 1734 at Muddy Creek, in the Conestoga
area of Lancaster County, Pennsylvania, the son of Mathias and
Catherine Spongh Ambrose. His baptism was recorded in the
records of the Rev. Stover as:- Joh. Philip Ambrosius, born
Feb. 6, 1734, baptized May 12, 1734, at Muddy Creek, son of
Matthias Ambrosius, sponsors, Philip and Susanna Schweikert.
   He was known as Philip and resided at Arnold's Delight, north
of Thurmont. Philip died in 1776 and the inventory of his
estate was dated August 31, 1776 and his wife Catherine was the
administratrix of his estate. He was probably interred at
Apple's Church Cemetery.
   Philip and his wife Eva Catherine were the parents of two
known children:-
1. HENRY(3) AMBROSE 1763-1845. Henry was born in 1763 near
   Thurmont. He was married to SOPHIA WEAVER, 1769-1841. They
   resided near Ellerton, Frederick County, Maryland and were
   interred at St. John's Lutheran Cemetery.
2. Maria Barbara Ambrose was born June 14, 1773, and was
   baptized July 21, 1773 at Apple's Church, the daughter of
   Philip and Eva Catherine Ambrose.

HENRY(3) AMBROSE 1763-1845.

Henry was born about 1763 near Thurmont, the son of Philip
and Eva Catherine Ambrose. He followed the trade of his grand-
father, Mathias, and was a farmer and miller.
   There were several Henry Ambroses listed in the Maryland
census from 1790 to 1840 who were residents of Frederick County.
They were most likely related and descended from Mathias.
Henry was listed in the Frederick County Assessment on land in
Lower and Middle Kittoctin Hundred. He is listed as Henry
Ambrozer of Philip, holding the patent to two tracts called
Neighbors Content of 68 acres and Stephen's Hope of 133 acres.
   Henry and his wife Sophia Weaver were members of the Lutheran
Church and their names appear in the records of Middletown Zion
and later in St. John's Lutheran Church at Ellerton. They were

interred at St. John's Lutheran Cemetery. The inscription from
their tombstone reads:- HENRY AMBROSE of PHILIP, died March 1845,
Aged 81 years 7 mos. & 19 days. SOPHIA wife of Henry Ambrose,
died 6 May 1841, Aged 72 Years 2 Mos. & 23 days.
    Henry and Sophia's daughter, Elizabeth Ambrose, 1791-1856, was
married to Philip Cline, 1786-1874. They resided in the Ellerton
area and were members of St. John's Lutheran Church. Elizabeth
and Philip were interred at St. John's Lutheran Cemetery.

BOARMAN

LINEAGE CHART
WILLIAM BOURMAN, m BARBARA WORSLEY.
WILLIAM(1) BOARMAN c 1625-1686, m c 1650, SARAH LINLE - SINLEY.
MARY(2) BOARMAN c 1660-1716, m c 1679, ROBERT GREENE.

WILLIAM(1) BOARMAN 1625-1686.
    The Boarman family of Maryland is of English descent and they
originated from Devonshire and Somersetshire, England. The
Maryland Boarmans share the same family crest as the Boarmans
of Wells, England.
    William Boarman was born about 1625 in England, the son of
William Bourman of Brooke and his wife Barbara Worsley. He was
brought into the Province of Maryland at the time of the civil
war in England by Captain Giles Brent. He resided with the
Jesuit priests at Port Tobacco where he received a catholic
education. During the 1645 Revolution he was among those
captured by adherents of Richard Ingle and taken prisoner to
St. Mary's City. By 1651 he was employed by Giles Brent on
Kent Island.
    William's home plantation in St. Mary's County was known as
Kitt Martins Point, which he sold in 1663 to James Jolly, an
inn keeper of St. Mary's for 15,000 pounds of tobacco. Of this
sum, half was to paid in St. Mary's County and the other half
in Charles County.
    In the 1660's William's land speculation included several
large tracts in Charles County. By 1676 these holdings were
consolidated into Boarman's Manor. The Manor extended several
miles on both sides of Zachiah Swamp with the northern most part
at present day Bryantown and included almost 4,000 acres.
    In 1678 William gave to his daughter Sarah Mudd, 450 acres of
Hall's Place, which adjoined her brother-in-law Robert Greene's,
on the north side of Green's Run into Zachiah Swamp. In 1679
William gave to his daughter Mary Green, Green's Rest which may
be the same as George's Rest. Robert Green's land is listed as
a reference in William Boarman's will of 1709 as being a part
of George's Rest. In 1755 Thomas Jameson requested boundaries
on Hall's Rest and George's Rest be proved. Joseph Jameson
referred to a dividing tree between the land of Mrs. Mudd and
Mrs. Green, the two sisters and daughters of Major William
Boarman.

During his lifetime, Major William Boarman was a mariner, a
captain and a major of the militia, planter, land speculator,
Indian trader and interpreter, sheriff and gentleman justice and
delegate to the General Assembly. He participated with the
Proprietary forces at the Battle of the Severn and the Nanticoke
Indian War of 1678. He was the ancestor of Francis Scott Key,
the author of 'The Star Spangled Banner', our national anthem.
His life is well documented in the early colonial records and
the Provincial Court records of Maryland. There were several
men in early Maryland with the name of William Boarman, including
his son and grandsons. But the early records must be attributed
to Major William Boarman of Boarman's Manor.
The only reference to William's death occurs in a petition of
resurvey of Boarman's Reserve. In 1755, Henry Mudd requested a
resurvey of his land called Boarman's Reserve, originally granted
to Major William Boarman, late of Charles County, being deceased
October 10, 1686.
William and his wife Sarah were the parents of five children:-
1. William Boarman, b c 1654, m1 Jane Neale, m 2 Mary Pile.
2. Sarah Boarman, b c 1656, d 1685, m 1 Thomas Matthews Jr.,
   m 2 1678, Thomas Mudd.
3. George Boarman, b c 1658, died young, and was never married.
4. MARY BOARMAN, b c 1660, d 1716, m c 1679, ROBERT GREENE,
   the son of THOMAS GREENE, the second Provincial Governor of
   Maryland.
5. Benjamin Boarman.

MARY BOARMAN GREENE   c 1660-1716.

Mary was born in St. Mary's County about 1660, the daughter of
Major William Boarman and his wife Sarah Sinley. She was married to her neighbor, Robert Greene, the son of Governor Thomas
Greene. In 1679 she received from her father, probably as a
dowry, the plantation St. George's Rest, which adjoined her
husband's plantation and her sister Sarah Mudd's home plantation
of Hall's Place.
By 1700 the Greene family had moved to the home plantation of
Greene's Inheritance, located on the Piscataway and Rowling
Roads. They probably sold their land holdings back to the Boar-
man family because they later appear in the records as a part
of Boarman's Manor.
It is believed that Robert died before 1706, for at that time
Mary bought Guyther's Purchase, located in St. Mary's County.
Mary died in 1716, a widow, and she had divided her home of
Guyther's Purchase between her sons Thomas and James Greene.
Robert and Mary were of the Catholic faith and were the
parents of eight children:-
1. Thomas Greene was born about 1683 and married Tecla Shircliff.
   He received a part of Guyther's Purchase from his mother's
   estate in 1716.
2. Elizabeth Greene was married to Alexander Hamilton of Charles
   County.

3. Mary Greene was married to John Thompson.
4. Sarah Greene was married to John Squires and Patrick Atee.
5. William Greene was born 1694.
6. Robert Greene died 1749.
7. Jane Greene Campbell.
8. JAMES GREENE I died in 1734 in Prince George's County. He
   was married to CHARITY HAGAN who died in 1754. James was
   the executor of his mother's will and received a part of
   Guyther's Purchase from his mother's estate in 1716. In
   1709 he inherited a part of the plantation known as Strife
   from his godfather Thomas Frederick of Prince George's
   County.

CARBAUGH

CHRISTIAN CARBAUGH   -1813, m SUSANNAH.
ELIZABETH 'BETSY' CARBAUGH, m JOHN 'JACOB' WILDASIN 1770-1822.
MARY ELIZABETH 'POLLY' WILDASIN 1816-1901, m JOHN GILLELAN.

According to family history the first Carbaugh was a Hessian
Soldier hired by England to fight in the Revolutionary War. On
his arrival in America he deserted the English army and settled
in York County, Pennsylvania.
    There is a Martin Karsbaugh listed in the Hessian Troops in
the American Revolution. He was in the Rall Regiment which
came to America in 1776 and was descended from Bulhorn, a
village near Kassell.
    The early tax and census records list a Martin Carbaugh as a
resident of Berwick Township, York County. His descendants
resided in York and Adams Counties, Pennsylvania and Frederick
County, Maryland.

CHRISTIAN CARBAUGH   -1813.
    Christian is listed in the tax and census records of York
County and later Franklin Township of Adams County. At one
time members of the Carbaugh family were large land owners of
Franklin Township.
    At the time of his death in 1813 Christian resided in Frank-
lin Township. His will was written October 2, 1813 and probated
November 27, 1813. He listed his wife Susannah and his children
and their inheritance:-
1. Adam Carbaugh and his brother Samuel inherited the home
   farm and grist mill.
2. John Carbaugh inherited a home in Franklin Township.
3. Martin Carbaugh inherited a home, lands, grist and saw mill
   in Franklin Township.
4. Christian Carbaugh inherited 300 acres.
5. Catherine Carbaugh, the wife of Abraham Surapan.
6. Eva Carbaugh, the wife of Henry Lauver.

7. Mary Carbaugh, the wife of Henry Pottoroff.
8. Christiana Carbaugh, the wife of John Carbaugh.
9. Elizabeth 'Betsy' Carbaugh, the wife of John Wilkeson (John 'Jacob' Wildasin).
10. Racheal Carbaugh, the wife of Henry Snyder.
11. Susannah Carbaugh, the wife of George Snyder.
   It appears that Christian was not in favor of three of his daughter's husbands. He placed Catherine, Christiana and Elizabeth's inheritance in trust and the interest thereof for the use of their children, until the deaths of their husbands.
   Christian and his family resided north west of Cashtown. Christian was interred at the Carbaugh family cemetery and his grave was marked by a fieldstone. The family cemetery was located in Franklin Township, near Mount Newman, now a part of Michaux State Forrest.

ELIZABETH 'BETSY' CARBAUGH WILDASIN.
   Elizabeth was known as Betsy and was the daughter of Christian and Susannah Carbaugh. She was married to John 'Jacob' Wildasin and resided at South Mountain, near Arendtsville. Betsy and her husband Jacob were interred at the Arendtsville Lutheran and Reformed Cemetery. They were the parents of four children:-
1. Samuel Wildasin.
2. Peter Wildasin.
3. MARY ELIZABETH 'POLLY' WILDASIN, 1811/16-1901. m 1 JOHN GILLELAN, m 2 Eli Ferguson.
4. Lydia Wildasin.

MARY ELIZABETH 'POLLY' WILDASIN GILLELAN FERGUSON 1811/16-1901.
   Mary was born about 1811/16 near Arendtsville, the daughter of John 'Jacob' Wildasin and his wife Elizabeth 'Betsy' Carbaugh. She was known as Polly and after the death of her parents she was placed in the guardianship of David Deardorff of Franklin Township.
   She was married to John Gillelan and resided near Emmitsburg, Frederick County, Maryland. After her first husband's death she married Eli Ferguson and resided at Friendscreek, Frederick County, Maryland. Polly died in 1901 and was interred beside her second husband at St. Anthony's Catholic Shrine Cemetery, Mt. St. Mary's, near Emmitsburg, Maryland.

DYER

LINEAGE CHART
PATRICK DYER   1680-1724, m 1702, COMFORT BARNES 1685-1760.
ELIZABETH DYER 1711-   , m 1727, JAMES GREENE II d 1776.
CATHERINE GREENE   1729-1808, m 1748, BASIL SPALDING   1719-1791.
HENRY SPALDING   1747-1816, m 1771, ANNE ELDER 1746-1806.

PATRICK DYER 1680-1724.

The Dyer family was from Heystburg in Wiltshire, England and Tottenham in North London. Patrick was born about 1680 in Maryland. His parents are unknown. He may have been the son of Thomas who emigrated in 1664.

Patrick and his wife, Comfort Barnes were members of the Church of England and were married on October 12, 1702 at the Piscataway Parish of Prince George's County. They were the parents of eight children who were born at Piscataway. Patrick died in 1724 and his estate was administered by Thomas Edelen. His widow Comfort later married Thomas Edelen.

At one time Thomas Edelen held the patents for over 5,000 acres of land at Piscataway. He died in 1749 and willed to his widow, Comfort the home plantation of Edelenton, during her life, and then to his god daughter, Comfort's granddaughter, Catherine Greene Spalding. He also gave 1900 acres to his brothers and his step-son Thomas Dyer. Also listed in his will were his step-daughters Elizabeth Greene and Sarah Saunders.

Comfort Barnes Dyer Edelen died in 1760. Her will was written May 10, 1760 and probated September 20, 1760. She lists her children, grandchildren, and great grandchildren, thus providing a genealogical record documenting the relationships of the Barnes, Dyer, Greene, and Spalding families.

Comfort's will is interesting due to the fact that it depicts the era in which she lived. Her will listed her descendants and the dispersal of her personal estate among them, including seven slaves. Her will, in part, reads as follows:- I Comfort Edelen of Prince George's County widow being sick and weak ... give to my son Edward Dyar my Negro Girl Sarah ... and furniture ... to my Daughter Penelope Howard my Negro Man Tom my best Bed & furniture & ... my wearing apparol ... to my Grandson Thomas Dyer son of Edward Dyar my ... Negro ... Joe & his wife Sarah & girl Nell & their Increase & one feathered bed & furniture ... unto my Grand daughter Ann Dyer Daughter of my son Edward Dyar my Negro Child Mary and her Increase ... unto my Grandson Thomas Edelen Green son of James Green my Negro Boy Joe ... unto my Great Grandchild Ann Spalding daught. of Bazil Spalding my Chest of Drawers & two cane back chairs ... unto my Grandchild Elizabeth Dyar Daughter of my son Thomas Dyar my Large Looking Glass ... unto my Daughter Elizabeth Green and Rebecca Sanders and the children of my son William Dyar Deceased ... 20 shillings ... equally divided ... my son Edward Dyar and my Daughter Penelope Howard Executor & Executrix.

Patrick and Comfort were the parents of eight children:-
1. Sarah Dyer, b 1703.
2. William Dyer, b 1706.
3. Penelope Dyer Howard, b 1709.
4. ELIZABETH DYER GREENE, b January 1, 1711, m July 26, 1727, JAMES GREENE.
5. Rebecca Dyer Saunders, b 1714.

6. Thomas Dyer, 1715-1768, m 1738, Henrietta Clements.
7. James Dyer, b 1717.
8. Edward Dyer, b 1719.

ELIZABETH DYER GREENE.

Elizabeth was born January 22, 1711 at Piscataway, Prince
George's County the daughter of Patrick and Comfort Barnes Dyer.
She was married on July 26, 1727, to James Greene and resided
on the home plantation called Strife located south of Piscataway
along the Mattawoman Creek.
Elizabeth and James were the parents of nine children:-
Catherine, Mary, Elizabeth, James, Rebecca, Thomas Edelen, Basil,
Charity and John. Their daughter, CATHERINE GREENE, 1729-1808,
was married in 1748 to BASIL SPALDING, 1719-1791. They resided
in Prince George's and Charles Counties. Catherine and Basil's
son, HENRY SPALDING was married to ANNE ELDER and moved to
Frederick County, Maryland.

ELDER

LINEAGE CHART
WILLIAM ELDER I   d 1714, m 1705, ELIZABETH FINCH c 1687-1729.
WILLIAM ELDER II   1707-1775, m 1742, JACOBA CLEMENTINA LIVERS.
ANNE ELDER 1746-1806, m 1771, HENRY SPALDING 1747-1816.

WILLIAM ELDER I   d 1714.

William, a Quaker immigrant from Lancashire, England, was
married in 1705 to Elizabeth Finch. Elizabeth was born about
1687 at Woodbridge, Calvert County, Maryland, the daughter of
Guy and Rebecca Finch.
William and Elizabeth resided at Goodwill, which was originally purchased in 1681 by Guy Finch. Goodwill was divided
between Guy's two daughters, Mary Finch Beavans and Elizabeth
Finch Elder. It was located north of and adjoined the home
plantation of Arnold Livers, known as Timberly. This area is
located south of Upper Marlboro, on Route 301 at Rosaryville
State Park.
William died in 1714 and his widow, Elizabeth was the administratrix of his estate. William and Elizabeth were the
parents of two sons:-
1. WILLIAM ELDER II, 1707-1775, was married first in 1728 to
   Ann Wheeler, 1709-1739, and married secondly in 1742 to
   JACOBA CLEMENTINA LIVERS, 1717-1807, the daughter of Arnold
   Livers of Prince George's County. They resided near Emmits-
   burg, Frederick County, Maryland.
2. Thomas Elder, 1709-c1769, was married to Hannah Rhiley and
   resided in Frederick County which later became Montgomery
   County.
In 1715 Elizabeth had married Solomon Stimton, a planter of
Prince George's County, and had one son Jeremiah Stimton.
Solomon died in 1726 and his estate was administered by his

widow Elizabeth. She received the land adjoining Charles Bevins
and his personal estate. His two step-sons, William and Thomas
Elder each received one cow and one calf.
By 1728 Elizabeth had married the third time to Peter Hoggins.
Elizabeth died in 1729 and Peter died in 1730.

WILLIAM ELDER II 1707-1775.
William was born in 1707 at Goodwill in Prince George's
County, the son of William and Elizabeth Finch Elder. His
father died in 1714 and by 1715 his mother had married Solomon
Stimton. In 1727 William received one cow and one calf from
his step-father's estate.
In 1728 William was among a party of Catholics, which on an
exploritory trip, traveled into the interior of Frederick
County. During the same year he had married Ann Wheeler, the
daughter of Richard Wheeler of Charles County. By 1732 he
received a patent for land in Frederick County. He cleared
the land and built a home before moving his young family to
Frederick County. He is listed in the 1733 census of Prince
George's County and in 1736 is listed on a deed between him and
Charles Beavans for the land called Goodwill.
By 1736 William had moved his family to their new home at the
foot of the Catoctin Spur of the Blue Ridge. His wife Ann died
on August 11, 1739 and William hollowed out a chestnut tree for
her coffin. Later her remains were transferred to the Elder
family cemetery.
On May 26, 1739, William received a patent for Slate Ridge
from Arnold Livers. On January 20, 1741, William purchased two
additional tracts of Beaverdam Level and Black Walnut Bottom.
By the November Court of 1741, William Elder became the overseer of the road from Catoctin Mountain to the wagon road near
Little Pipe Creek. Originally it was a part of the Carledge's
Old Road, now known as Kelbaugh's Road. At that time William
resided on Slate Ridge on Little Owen's Creek about one mile
south of Saint Anthony's.
On February 2, 1742, William was married to Jacoba Clementina
Livers, the daughter of Arnold Livers and his wife Hellen
Gordon. Jacoba was born in 1717 at the Livers home plantation
of Timberly in Prince George's County, which adjoined the
Elder home of Goodwill. Beside the Livers home of Timberly,
Arnold owned several large tracts in Frederick County. On
August 24, 1743, William purchased from Arnold Livers, a part
of Ogle's Good Will, which became their new home. William
called his new home Pleasant Level but was better known as
Elder's Station. Here William built his new home and reserved
one room for a chapel. This chapel was for family use and
later served the Catholics of the area until 1808 when Mount
Saint Mary's Church on the hill was erected.

On April 11, 1775, William died of pneumonia at his home of
Pleasant Level. He was interred beside his first wife at the
Elder Cemetery. During his lifetime he had aquired over 1200
acres of land in the Emmitsburg district of Frederick County.
He is attributed with being the first white settler and estab-
lishing the first home for the Catholic faith in the region.
Mount Saint Mary's College was founded on what was originally
William Elder's property and bears the name he gave to the area.
   His widow, Jacoba, remained at the Elder homestead. She is
listed in the 1790 census as head of the household with one male,
one female and six slaves. On September 19, 1807, Jacoba died at
the age of 90 years and her funeral mass was held at Mount Saint
Mary's Church. She was interred beside her husband at the family
cemetery near the home where she had lived for 65 years.
   William and Ann were the parents of five children:-
1. William Elder III, 1729-1804, m 1752, Sabina Wickham. They
   resided near Emmitsburg and were interred at the Elder family
   cemetery.
2. Charles Elder, 1730-1804, m 1760, Julia Ward. They resided
   near Emmitsburg.
3. Guy Elder, 1732-1805, ml Eleanor Wickham Beale, m2 Eleanor
   Ogle Willett. They resided near Emmitsburg.
4. Richard Elder, 1734-1790, m Pheobe Deloyzier. They resided
   near Emmitsburg.
5. Mary Elder, 1735-1798, m 1755, Richard Lilly, d 1792.
   Mary and Richard were interred at Mount Pleasant.
   William and Jacoba were the parents of seven children:-
1. Elizabeth Elder, 1743-1820, m 1760, Richard Brawner.
   They resided near Emmitsburg.
2. Arnold Elder, 1745-1812, m Clotilda Pheobe Green, 1752-1833.
   Clotilda was married a second time to Roger Brooke and
   resided near Emmitsburg.
3. ANN ELDER, 1746-1806, m 1771, HENRY SPALDING, the son of
   BASIL and CATHERINE GREENE SPALDING. They resided near
   Taneytown and were interred at Taneytown St. Joseph's
   Catholic Cemetery.
4. Thomas H. Elder, 1748-1832, m 1771, Elizabeth Spalding, the
   daughter of Basil and Catherine Greene Spalding. They lived
   at Harbaugh Valley and later moved to Nelson County,
   Kentucky.
5. Ignatius Elder, 1749-c1800, Soldier of the American Revolution. He was married to Elizabeth Brawner and moved to
   Kentucky.
6. Francis Elder, 1756-1809, Soldier of the American Revolution.
   He was married to Catherine Spalding, the daughter of Basil
   and Catherine Greene Spalding. They resided in Frederick
   County and were interred at the Elder Cemetery.
7. Aloysius Elder, 1757-1827, ml Elizabeth Mills, 1757-1802,
   m2 Mary Josephine Green Hayden, 1775-1842. They lived at
   the Elder homestead and were interred at the Elder Cemetery.

William's tombstone was quarried from the local stone and the
inscription was carved by his sons. Ann's tombstone is believed
to be the oldest in the Emmitsburg area. Jacoba's tombstone was
broken into several pieces and was reinforced. In 1878 another
marker was erected by Archbishop William Henry Elder, and marked
the location of the Elder home and chapel. Several years ago
the original markers were removed to the Marylandia Collection
of Mount Saint Mary's College and were replaced by marble markers.
The inscriptions from these markers reads as follow:-
1. Here remains the body of William Elder Senior, - Born in the
   year 1707, - Aged 68 Departed April 22d 1775 and awaits the
   resurrection of the just May they rest in peace amen.
2. Here Remains The Body of Ann Wheeler, first wife of William
   Elder Senior Departed this life August the 6th, 1739, Aged
   30 years.
3. In memory of Jacoba Clemin---, wife of William ----r died
   Sept--- 1807 Aged 90 y--rs.
4. Nearby was erected by William Elder, Sr., the first altar to
   the Living God in what is now known as Mt. St. Mary, Emmitsburg & Mechanicstown Congregations, about the year 1745.
   This stone was erected by his descendants 103 years after his
   death. Here remains the body of ANN WHEELER first wife of
   William Elder, Sr., Departed this life August 11, 1739 Aged
   30 years. Here remains the body of William Elder, Senior,
   Born in the year 1707 Aged 68 Departed April 22, 1775 and
   awaits the resurrection of the just. May he rest in peace.
   Amen. In memory of Jacoba Clementina wife of William Elder
   Sr. Died Sept 19, 1807, Aged 90 years.

ANNE ELDER SPALDING 1746-1806.

Anne was born in 1746 at the Elder home near Emmitsburg, the
daughter of William and Jacoba Clementina Livers Elder. In 1771
Anne was married at the Conewago Catholic Chapel, near Hanover,
Pennsylvania, to Henry Spalding, the son of Basil and Catherine
Greene Spalding of Charles County, Maryland.
   In 1776 she is listed in her father's will as Anne Spalding.
She received one Negro Girl named Cate, one Cow and calf, two
ewes and lambs, one feathered bed and bed clothes and ten
pounds Pennsylvania currency.
   After their marriage, Anne and Henry resided in Charles and
Prince George's Counties. By the 1780's they resided at their
home farm Addition to Brooke's Discovery, a 545 acre farm on
the Monocacy River, between Emmitsburg and Taneytown. Here
they raised their eight children.
   Ann died on January 17, 1806 and Henry died ten years later
on February 19, 1816. They were interred at Taneytown St.
Joseph's Catholic Cemetery.

FINCH

LINEAGE CHART
GUY FINCH   -1688, m REBECCA.
ELIZABETH FINCH c1687-1729, m 1705, WILLIAM ELDER I,   -1714.

GUY FINCH   -1688.
Guy immigrated from England to Maryland in 1674 on board the
ship Dover. In 1681 he purchased 100 acres called Goodwill and
in 1684 he purchased an additional 118 acres called Woodbridge.
Both tracts were located in Calvert County a few miles south of
the town of Upper Marlboro. By 1696 this part of Calvert County
became Prince George's County.
Guy and his wife Rebecca were the parents of two daughters:-
1. Mary Finch was married to Charles Beavens and resided at
   Goodwill.
2. ELIZABETH FINCH was married to WILLIAM ELDER, Soloman
   Stimton, and Peter Hoggins and resided at Goodwill.
Guy died in 1688 and his widow, Rebecca was administratrix of
his estate. The home plantation of Goodwill was equally divided
between his two young daughters, Mary and Elizabeth. Rebecca
remained at Woodbridge and later married Henry Culver, a
Catholic of English descent. In 1693 Rebecca and her husband
Henry were the administrators of the final account of Guy Finch.
His estate was valued at 57 pounds sterling and 11,407 pounds
of tobacco. By 1694 Rebecca had signed over Woodbridge to Henry
Darnal, who signed it over to Henry Culver.
Rebecca and Henry were the parents of one son, Henry Culver,
Jr. Rebecca died about 1712 and Henry was married to Catherine
Beavens and were the parents of seven children.

ELIZABETH FINCH ELDER STIMTON HOGGINS c1687-1729.
Elizabeth was born about 1687 at Goodwill, the daughter of
Guy and Rebecca Finch. Elizabeth and her sister Mary inherited
their father's home of Goodwill, which was equally divided
between them. In 1705 Elizabeth was married to William Elder I,
a Quaker immigrant from Lancashire, England. They resided at
Goodwill and were the parents of two sons, Thomas and William
Elder.
After her husband William Elder's death in 1714, Elizabeth
was married to Soloman Stimton and had one son Jeremiah Stimton.
After Soloman's death in 1726, Elizabeth was married a third
time to Peter Hoggins. Elizabeth died in 1729 and her husband
Peter died the following year.
Both of Elizabeth's sons, Thomas and William Elder, settled
in Frederick County. William was known as an early settler of
the Emmitsburg district. With him came the Catholic Church into
the area and his children and grandchildren were among the
pioneers who settled in Kentucky. So through her descendants,
Elizabeth became the ancestor of a family of pioneers who moved
this country westward.

LINEAGE CHART
JOHN VALENTINE FLOHR 1726-1804, m 1746, ELIZABETH ZIMMERMAN.
LEONARD FLOHR I 1750-1820, m ANNA MARGREDA 1750-1804.
LEONARD FLOHR II 1773-1840, m RACHEAL SMITH 1778-1850.
WILLIAM FLOHR 1798-1854, m 1824, SUSAN HAFLEIGH 1800-1894.
MARIA ANN FLOHR 1832-1919, m 1855, BENJAMIN SHRINER 1832-1865.

The name originated from the Spanish Flores which means
flowers. It is of German and Swedish background and has had
several transformations of Flowers, Flor, Flore, Flohr, and
many other variations.
At this time research indicates that the emigrant ancestor of
the family was Conrad Flohr. He was born in 1690 in Germany
and emigrated from Rotterdam to the port of Deal, England and
arrived at Philadelphia on September 3, 1739. He is listed
among the Palatines imported on the ship Friendship as Conrade
Flowers, age 49, also listed are Mich'l Flowers, age 25, and
Leonard Flowers, age 28. They are also listed on the ship
passenger list as Conrad Florans, Micheal Floris, and Leonhart
Floor.

JOHN VALENTINE FLOHR 1726-1804.
John Valentine was born in 1726 in Germany, and believed to
be the son of Conrad Flohr. He was thirteen years old when his
family emigrated and since only men above the age of sixteen
are listed on the ship passenger list, his name does not appear
in any of the records.
He followed the German custom of using his middle name after
he reached maturity. He was known as Valentine and his name
appears in the records as Velte, Vete, and Velter.
Valentine was married three times, his first wife is unknown,
his second wife was Elizabeth Zimmerman, and his third wife was
another Elizabeth. They resided near the small town of Dover,
York County, Pennsylvania. Valentine owned 150 acres in Dover
Township. His land was the subject of a lawsuit in the summer
of 1786. There was some adverse possession claim by Charles
Albert on which the court denied and ordered a patent to
Valentine Flohr.
Strayer's Church now known as Salem's Church, was established
May 30, 1757 and was located near the town of Dover. Valentine
was among the 28 members of the Reformed and Lutheran congregation which founded this church. Valentine and his son Leonard
appear on the tax lists of Dover Township for the years 1762
and 1771.
His second wife, Elizabeth Zimmerman, was born February 28,
1724. She was the daughter of George Zimmerman, of Gallberg
near Heidelberg, Germany. Elizabeth's family were passengers
on the ship Neptune which arrived at Philadelphia on October
25, 1746. Elizabeth died on March 14, 1775 at the age of 51
and was interred at Strayer's Church Cemetery. The inscription
from her tombstone, which is in German, reads:- HIER. RVHET
ELIESABETHA FLORIN, 1ST GEBOR REN YAHR 1724 GESTORBEN DEN 14
MERTZ 1775.

Valentine's will was written July 30, 1803 and was probated in 1804. He listed his wife as Elizabeth, and his children, Leonard, Susanna, wife of Peter Yeges, Ann Margaret, wife of Adam Yeges, Elizabeth, wife of Jacob Banters, Valentine Jr., and Anna Mary. The executors of his estate were John Sharp and John Crone and his estate had a balance of over 1701 pounds. On March 27, 1805, his widow Elizabeth, selected Charles Mittman as guardian of her children Valentine and Margaret Flohr.

John Valentine Flohr was the father of 9 children:-
1. LEONARD FLOHR I, 1750-1820. He was married to Anna Margreda and they resided near Dover and later near Arendtsville.
2. John George Flohr, 1754-1764. Johann Georg Flor was born April 24, 1754 and died September 5, and was buried September 6, 1764 at Strayer's Cemetery near Dover. According to the church records he was the son of Vete and Elizabeth Flor.
3. Susanna Flohr, the daughter of Belte Flohr, was married January 30, 1770 to Peter Yeges (Jeki).
4. Mary Elizabeth Flohr was born May 13, 1763 and baptised June 19, 1763, at Strayer's Church, the daughter of Velter and Elizabeth Flohr. According to her father's will she was married to Jacob Banters.
5. Anna Maria Flohr, daughter of Velto Flohr, was married at Strayer's Church on September 3, 1771, to John Adam Yeges (Jeki).
6. Jacob Flohr.
7. David Flohr.
8. Valentine Flohr, Jr.
9. Margaret Flohr.

LEONARD FLOHR I 1750-1820.

Leonard was born in 1750 near Dover, the son of John Valentine and Elizabeth Zimmerman Flohr. He is listed in the 1762 and 1771 tax lists of Dover Township. He was a soldier of the American Revolution and is listed as Lenhart Florey in Captain Christian Coffman's Company of Dover Township.

Leonard and his family resided in the Dover area until the mid 1780s at which time they moved near the town of Arendtsville in Franklin Township. On June 14, 1787, Leonard purchased 180 acres on the road from Paxtang to Monocacy and purchased another 200 acres on October 26, 1796. In this area is the small village of Floradale which may have been named after the Flohr family.

Leonard and his wife were members of Strayer's Church and later members of the Lutheran and Reformed Church at Arendtsville. Anna Margreda was born in 1750 and died in 1804. She was interred at the Arendtsville Lutheran and Reformed Cemetery and later moved to the Flohr family plot at Flohr's Church Cemetery near McKnightstown.

Leonard wrote his will on November 29, 1814, but sometime
after that date he moved to Columbia County, Ohio, where he died
in 1820. His will was probated on January 10, 1821 and his
estate was equally divided among his 8 living children, Leonard,
Frederick, Valentine, Samuel, Daniel, Jacob, and Sarah who had
married David Mickley, and his two grandsons, John and Joseph,
heirs of Joseph Flohr, deceased son of Leonard. At the time of
his death he still owned mountain land in Franklin Township.
The final account balance of his estate was $9,813.61, and was
administered by his son Valentine Flohr on May 23, 1826.
Leonard and Anna Margreda Flohr were the parents of nine
children:-
1. LEONARD FLOHR II, 1773-1840. He was born September 18, 1773
   near Dover and died June 26, 1840, near Fairfield. He was
   married to Racheal Smith, 1778-1850, and they were interred
   at Elias Lutheran Cemetery, Emmitsburg, Frederick County,
   Maryland.
2. Samuel Flohr. Samuel was born April 16, 1786 and baptized
   June 18, 1786, at the Arendtsville Lutheran Church, the son
   of Lahnart and Anna Margretha Flohr. The sponsors at his
   baptism were Philip and Anna Margaretha Schaffer.
3. Daniel Flor was born August 2, 1789 and baptized May 9, 1790,
   the son of Leonh and Margaret Flor. The sponsors at his
   baptism were Nic. and Elizabeth Barbara Bissecker.
4. Frederick Flohr.
5. Valentine Flohr.
6. Joseph Flohr.
7. David Flohr.
8. Jacob Flohr.
9. Sarah Flohr was married to David Mickley.

LEONARD FLOHR II   1773-1840.
Leonard was born September 18, 1773, near Dover, the son of
Leonard and Anna Margreda Flohr. He was baptized October 31,
1773 at Strayer's Church and his grandparents, Velte and
Elizabeth Zimmerman Flohr were the baptism sponsors.
Leonard and his wife Racheal Smith resided near Arendtsville
and were members of the Lutheran Church. Several of their
children were baptized at the Lutheran and Reformed Church of
Arendtsville.
By 1800 they had moved to the Fountaindale area of south-
western Liberty Township. They are listed in the 1800 census
as Leonard Floore, with 5 males and 4 females in the Flohr
household. Leonard is listed in the land records of Adams
County and had several transactions in Franklin, Liberty, and
Hamiltonban Townships from 1805 to 1839. One of these land
transactions was on April 11, 1839, at which time he sold land
in Liberty Township to his son William.

The Flohr home farm was located on the northern side of Raven Rock Mountain at Cove Hollow. At this time members of the Flohr family owned most of the land in this area from Jack's Mountain Road to Zora.

Leonard wrote his will on May 11, 1840 and it was probated on August 3, 1840. He provided for his wife, but her name is not listed. He empowered his executors, his son John Flohr and son-in-law Samuel Beard, to sell his real estate and personal estate at a public sale. The proceeds were equally divided between his children, William, John, Jacob, David, Rhueben, Lydia Ann, the wife of Henry Layman, and Elizabeth, the wife of Samuel Beard. His estate sale was listed in the Sentinel newspaper of Gettysburg on August 10, 1840.

While they resided at Cove Hollow, Leonard and Racheal and their family were members of Elias Lutheran Church, Emmitsburg, Frederick County, Maryland. They were interred at Elias Lutheran Cemetery and the inscription from their tombstone reads:- In memory of Leonard Flohr born September 18th 1773 and departed this life June 26, 1840, Aged 67 Years, 9 months and 8 days. In memory of Racheal Flohr, Wife of Leonard Flohr, who departed this life January 15th 1850, Aged 72 Years.

Leonard and Racheal Smith Flohr were the parents of 10 children:-
1. Lydia Ann Flohr. Lythea was born June 7, 1796 and baptized July 31, 1796, at the Arendtsville Lutheran Church, the daughter of Leonhardt and Rechel Flor. The sponsors of her baptism were her grandparents Leonhardt and Margaretha Flor. Lydia was married to Henry Layman.
2. WILLIAM FLOHR 1798-1854. Wilhelm Flor was born January 21, 1798 and baptized March 14, 1798, at the Arendtsville Lutheran Church, the son of Leonh. and Rahel Flor. The sponsor of his baptism was his uncle Valentine Flor. He was married to Susan Hafleigh.
3. Elizabeth Flor was born July 26, 1799 and baptized September 15, 1799 at the Arendtsville Lutheran Church, the daughter of Leonhardt and Rahel Flor. Elizabeth was married to Samuel Beard.
4. Rev. John Flohr. Johannes Flor was born December 14, 1802 and baptized at the Arendtsville Lutheran Church, the son of Leonhardt and Rahel Flor. He was married to Amanda Green and resided near Fountaindale. They were the parents of 10 children, Jenny, Charles, Ann, Simon Peter, Fanny Gantz, Harvey, Benton, Mart, Aunt Dean, and Jess Flohr.
5. Samuel Flohr.
6. Rev. Charles Flohr.
7. Rhueben Flohr.
8. Leonard Flohr III.
9. David Flohr.
10. Jacob Flohr.

WILLIAM FLOHR   1798-1854.
William was born January 21, 1798, near Arendtsville and was
baptized March 14, 1798 at the Arendtsville Lutheran Church,
the son of Leonh and Rahel Flor. The sponsor of his baptism
was Valentine Flor, who was probably his uncle.
According to the Compiler newspaper records of Gettysburg,
William Flore and Susannah Haefleigh, both of Adams County, were
married on September 14, 1824, by the Rev. David Bossler. They
are listed in the 1850 census of Liberty Township as William, a
farmer, and his wife Susan, and children, Ann E., Catherine,
Ann M., Racheal S., Mitilda, Mary Jane, and Sarah.
William's farm was located on the northeastern slope of Raven
Rock Mountain near Zora. He resided here for some time before
he purchased this farm from his father in 1839.
William and his family were members of Elias Lutheran Church
at Emmitsburg. William died on April 4, 1854 of pneumonia at
his home farm. According the the Flohr - Hardman Family bible,
which was the bible of Racheal Smith Flohr Hardman, William was
born January 21, 1798 and died March 4, 1854. His wife Susan
Hafleigh Flohr was born August 6, 1800 and died May 24, 1894, at
the age of 93 years. William and Susan were interred at the
Lutheran Cemetery at Emmitsburg. The inscription from their
tombstones reads, William Flohr, Born Jan 21st 1798, Died March
4th 1854, Aged 56 Years 1 mo. and 11 days. SUSAN, wife of
William Flohr, Died May 24, 1894, Aged 93 yrs. 9 mos.
Susan was a lifetime member of Elias Lutheran Church. She was
baptized in 1800 by the Rev. John G. Grobp, a minister of the
Emmitsburg church. In 1892 she was listed as the oldest member
of the congregation. Her obituary appeared in the Gettysburg
newspaper on June 5, 1894. According to her obituary, Mrs.
Susan Flohr, widow of the late William Flohr, died at her home
in Liberty Township on May 24, 1894, at the age of 93 years.
She is thought to have been the oldest resident of that
community and lived in the house which she died for about sixty
years. She had been in a helpless condition and her eye sight
was quite dim, at times being almost blind. The deceased was
the mother of nine children, and had 23 grandchildren and 19
great grandchildren.
William and Susan were the parents of 10 children:-
1. Eliza Flohr was born in 1826 and was married to Franklin
   McKissick.
2. Catherine Flohr was born in 1828 and was married to Jahua
   Hardman.
3. Lydia Lucinda Flohr, 1830-1833. She was interred at the
   Lutheran Cemetery, Emmitsburg, Maryland.
4. Valentine Flohr, 1831-1831. Valentine died of measles and
   was interred at the Lutheran Cemetery, Emmitsburg, Maryland.
5. MARIA ANN FLOHR, 1832-1919. Maria was married in 1855 to
   Benjamin Shriner, 1832-1865, the son of Peter and Sarah
   Shriner of Friendscreek, Frederick County, Maryland.

6. Racheal Smith Flohr, 1836-1921. She was named after her grandmother and in 1872 she was married to George W. Hardman. They were interred at Fountaindale Union Cemetery.
7. Sarah A. Flohr, 1839-1879. Sarah was interred at Emmitsburg Lutheran Cemetery.
8. Mitilda Flohr, 1841-1863. Mitilda was born November 16, 1841 and was baptized April 23, 1842, at the Trinity Lutheran Church, Taneytown, the daughter of William and Susan Flohr. She died at the age of 21 and was interred at the Emmitsburg Lutheran Cemetery.
9. Mary Jane Flohr, 1844-1878. Mary Jane was married in 1866 to Charles E. Wetzel, 1843-1920. They were the parents of three children, William Oliver Wetzel, Maria Estella Wetzel Zimmerman, and John McClain Wetzel. Mary Jane died in 1878 and was interred at Emmitsburg Lutheran Cemetery.
10. Rebecca Flohr, 1847-1873. Rebecca was married to Abraham C. Myers, and were the parents of Sidney and Daniel. Rebecca and her third child died in 1873 and were interred at Emmitsburg Lutheran Church Cemetery. Abraham's second wife was Sarah Amanda Hoover, the daughter of John and Mary Ann Overholtzer Hoover, of Liberty Township.

MARIA ANN FLOHR SHRINER   1832-1919.
According to the records of the Trinity Lutheran Church of Taneytown, Maryland, Maria was born on December 9, 1843 and baptized on June 16, 1844, the daughter of William and Susan Hafleigh Flohr. But according to the Civil War Pension Records, she gave the date of her birth as February 9, 1832.

Maria was married on February 13, 1855, at the Elias Lutheran Church in Emmitsburg to Benjamin Shriner, the son of Peter and Sarah Shriner of Friendscreek. Shortly after their marriage they resided on the farm next door to Maria's mother.

Benjamin was a veteran of the Civil War and died on June 5, 1865 at Campbell Hospital, Washington D.C. He was interred at Arlington National Cemetery and a tombstone was erected in his memory at the Shriner family plot at Friendscreek Cemetery.

Maria and her children remained at the Shriner home near Zora. They are listed in the census records of 1870 to 1910. Maria is also listed in the 1872 Atlas of Adams County as Mrs. Shriner, Liberty Township, and resided on the northeastern side of Raven Rock Mountain.

Maria collected a pension from the government for the service of her husband during the Civil War. These records contain a lot of family information. Her children are listed as Uriah Augustus Shriner and Rena Shriner and her signature is listed as Maria A. Shriner. According to these records, Maria died on May 25, 1919 and was interred at the Shriner family plot at the Friendscreek Cemetery. Her grave was simply marked with a fieldstone and a marble marker with the inscription M.S.

Benjamin and Maria were the parents of two children:-
1. Uriah Augustus Shriner, 1857-1901. Uriah was married in
   1885 to Jennie M. Stayley and resided near Fairfield. They
   were interred at St. Mary's Catholic Cemetery, Fairfield.
   They were the parents of 4 children, Charles Shriner, who
   died young, Charles Augustus, Ada, of Chambersburg, Bessie,
   who married Preston Sanders, and Lawrence Shriner, who
   married Ethel Mull.
2. IRENE HESTER SHRINER, 1862-1937. She was known as Rena and
   was born May 1, 1862 at the Shriner home near Zora. In 1898
   she was married to George Basil Gilland, the son of John and
   Victoria Spalding Gilland of Emmitsburg, Maryland. Rena
   died at the place of her birth on October 17, 1937. She was
   a lifelong resident of the Fairfield area. George and Rena
   were members of the Lutheran Church and later the Greenstone
   Apostolic Church and were interred at Fairfield Union Cemetery.
   They were the parents of 6 children, Bertie L. McCleaf Gilland,
   Arthur B., John E., Mary E., James Henry, and Charles Benjamin
   Gilland.

GILLAND

THE BACKGROUND OF THE GILLILAND FAMILY

A study of the name becomes quite involved in a variety of
spellings, meanings, and origins. Some of the early spellings
barely resemble the present day form.

The Irish origin of gillian or gaillian, which means the little
youth, has been spelled various ways and claims an origin of
87 B.C. Other forms are from giolla, meaning lad, took the form
of O'Giollain, Giollain, Gilland, Gillan, O'Gillegan, and
Gilligan.

Some of the Scottish surnames as in the similiar Irish
practice embody the term gille. Many variations of spelling
gave form to guill, gilla, gilli, an ancient Gaelic expression
meaning disciple, follower, or servant. Gille is also of the
Norse Gilla from Ole Gilla meaning servant.

In Scotland the name is derived from the Gaelic MacGille
S'Fhaolain or MacGill'Fhaolin, meaning son of the servant of
St. Fillan, a popular saint in ancient times. Through several
transformations it took the forms of MacGillychallin, McGillo-
lane, McGillelan. Later the Mac was omitted and simply became
Gillelan, Gilliland, and Gillalin to those of the Presbyterian
faith, and Gilland to those of Catholic extraction. It simply
meant son of Gill'sland.

These names were connected with the clan McClean, from the
Gaelic Gill Evin, meaning servant of St. John. Another descent
both MacKenzies and Macleans is from Gilleoin of the Aird. The
Macleans and Gillelan clans lived in northwestern Scotland on
the Isle of Mull.

From another source, Gillelan is considered a popular name in
Scotland and means servant of the land. It is derived from two
forms into one. The first is Gille, derived from the latin
Julius, originally meaning the devine. The second half is lan,
short form of land. This part of the name usually referred to
the estate of a chief or king. This suggests that the Gillelans
were at one time associated with the royal family.

Another theory of origin traces the background to Bueth Mac
Gille, Lord of Galway of Scotland. He was also the Baron of
Gilleslandia, which was one of the original baronies of Cumbria
in southern Scotland, now a part of England. It was known as
the barony of Gilleslandia, Gillesland, Gill'slan, and Gilsland.
Today the English medival town of Gilsland, located on Hadrian's
Wall, on the border of Cumberland and Northumberland Counties,
may be all that remains of the barony of Gilleslandia.

One branch of the family trace their genealogy back to the
highlands of Scotland. William 'Willy' Gilliland took part in
the Battle of 1676, between the King of England and the Scots.
The King won and Willy fled for his life to Northern Ireland.

His adventure and flight from Scotland has been recorded in
'Willy Gilliland - An Ulster Ballad, from Lays of the Western
Gael and Other Poems.' This epic was written by Sir Samuel
Ferguson, whose grandmother was Ellen Gilliland, a descendant of
Willy Gilliland.

According to English tradition the name was originally guilli,
Guill, and gilli and were servants in the royal household. Later
members of the family became mercenery soldiers for the King of
England. For their service to the crown they were granted land
in southern Scotland and northern England and the name became
known as Gilliland. It was already established in England prior
to the Battle of Hastings in 1066. This tradition can be adapted
to the Scottish tradition of Bueth MacGille, Lord of Galway and
Baron of Gilleslandia.

Although the origin of the name has been traced through history
and lost to antiquity, it is most definately of Gaelic - Celtic
background. Over the centuries the name has had several
transformations and has been dispersed throughout the British
Isles. The name has been recorded in England, Wales, the Isles
of Man, Scotland and Ireland.

Early in the 18th century members of the family emigrated to
America. They arrived at the main ports of New York, New
Jersey, Pennsylvania, Maryland, South Carolina, and have been
dispersed throughout the United States. The name has continued
in the most common form of Gilliland, as well as Gilleland,
Gilleylen, Gillelan, Gilland, and any variation thereof.

THE EARLY GILLILANDS OF FREDERICK COUNTY

Members of the Gilliland family appear in the early records of Frederick County from its formation in 1748. Before that date they are listed in the records of Prince George's County, of which was divided and the western part became Frederick County. Most of this early information is from the land, court, and tax records. Relationship has not been established from these early records. However, since they lived in the same area they were most likely related. At a later date, other Gilliland family members moved into Frederick County. Their relationship, if any, to the early Gillilands, remains unknown.

We find the names of Hugh, James, John, Thomas, William, Jane, Hannah, and Mary, quite common names of the Gilliland family, which have been used in each succeeding generation. Therefore, this repetition of names makes it difficult to determine with any accuracy what information refers to who. The names have been recorded as they appear in the original documents.

HUGH GILLILAND

In the Prince George's County Court of 1739, Evan Shelby, Sr., Evan Shelby, Jr., and Hugh Gilleland were forced to pay the Rev. William Williams the 90 pounds sterling and 486 pounds of tobacco which they owed him. In the August Court of 1750 of Frederick County the Rev. Williams sued Hugh Gilliland for a debt of 10 pounds. Again in the March Court of 1751 the Rev. Williams sued Gilliland for his failure to pay his debt and was charged the cost of the court.

From 1743 to 1745, Hugh was the overseer of roads from Conococheque to Licking Creek. In 1745 he purchased 50 acres of land called Security, near Green Springs, now Washington County. In 1748 a road was laid out from Conococheque to Hugh Gillilans.

Hugh Gilliland, of Prince George's County, farmer, was one of the Sureties in the will of Joseph Erwin dated March 26, 1748, and again in the will of William Griffith. In 1749 Hugh purchased 790 acres of land called Resurvey on Hazard. By 1750 Hugh was a member of the jury in the Frederick County June Court. The same year he purchased 150 acres called Big Spring.

In 1774 a Hugh Gilliland was appointed Constable for Conocochque Hundred. In 1779 Hugh Gilliland of Washington County, farmer, sold to Richard Barnes of St. Mary's County, Beall's Fort on the banks of the Potomac. In the same year he purchased 100 acres called Indian Bottom on the Potomac.

By 1784 a Hugh Gilliland, of Virginia, sold Indian Bottom to Thomas and James Prather of Washington County, Maryland. Indian Bottom was originally granted to Thomas Gilliland.

JAMES GILLILAND
    In 1750 James Gilliland purchased 150 acres of land called
Big Spring, now Washington County. By 1755 and 1756 he is
listed in the Debt Books, a tax list, for Big Spring and Beall's
Fort. He served as a juror for the March and June Court of
1753. He witnessed and proved the will of George Pack of
Frederick County in 1753 and 1754.
    He appeared in the November Court of 1754 along with other
inhabitants of Frederick County, requesting a road to Gilliland's
Mill. He is also listed as one of the sureties in the will of
James Jack in 1754.
    James had died by 1757 at which time an inventory of his
estate was valued at over 23 pounds. Mary Gilliland, her
relationship unknown, swore an oath to a just and perfect inventory. James' estate remained in the court for the next ten years.
Hannah Gilliland was appointed administratrix of his estate.
According to these records she married William Polk and the final
account of James' esate was received in the September Court in
1767.

THOMAS GILLILAND
    Thomas appears in the records as early as 1749 at which time
he operated Gililan's Mill near Clear Spring. By 1752 he had
purchased 100 acres of Indian Bottom on the Potomac.
    In 1753 Joseph Chapline, son-in-law of the Rev. Williams, sued
Thomas Gilliland in court. Thomas was deceased by 1768 and his
heirs are listed as rent due on the lands of Thomas Gilliland.
In 1784 a Hugh Gilliland of Virginia sold Indian Bottom, which
was granted to Thomas Gilliland in 1752.

WILLIAM GILLILAND
    A William Gillens is listed in the 1733 Taxables of Potomac
Hundred, of Prince George's County, now a part of Frederick
County. In 1750 he purchased 100 acres of land called Darlings
Delight from Thomas Cresap and was also the overseer of roads
in Conocheque Hundred. By 1753 a William Gilliland was the
witness to the will of Charles Polk of Frederick County. In
1754 he was overseer of the road from Fifteen Mile Creek to
Great Tonoloway.
    William Gilliland appears in the Debt Book, a tax list for
Darlings Delight of Frederick County for the years 1755 to 1757.
According to these records, Darlings Delight was on the west
side of South Mountain. Also listed for the same area was James
and Thomas Gilliland.
    On December 23, 1756, a William Gilliland was shot and scalped
on the east side of Fort Frederick. He had been with a detach-
ment under Ensign Prather. He was still alive when found on the
Thomson plantation, but nothing could be done to save his life.
William's will was written on May 16, 1756 and probated January
19, 1758. He gave his estate to his wife Mary Gilliland, who
was the executrix of his estate.

Further research indicates that members of this family moved
to Virginia, West Virgina, and Ohio. One branch of the family
intermarried into the family of Daniel Boone.

EVIDENCE OF THE GILLILAND FAMILY IN FREDERICK COUNTY.

Evidence of the family can be found in Frederick County for
the last two and a half centuries. Several members of the
family appear in the records a few times and then disappear
from the paper trail. At times several different individuals
with the same name lived in the same area at the same time.
Due to this fact it is difficult to determine who's who.
One such case is Philip Gillion who was married in 1787 to
Catherine Rowe. A Philip Gilleland is listed in the 1790 Census.
Another Philip Gillion arrived in Frederick County in 1794 and
appeared on the Presidential Election Poll of 1796.
A Peter Gillelan was the administrator of John Gilleylen's
estate in 1784 and 1785. At the same time Peter Gillylen is
recorded in the Baltimore newspaper records as residing near
Taneytown. At first he refused to pay the debts of his wife
Margaret. But later he assumed the responsibility of his wife's
debts.
A Margaret Gilleland is listed as a member of Tom's Creek
Presbyterian Church. She resided in Emmitsburg and owned a lot
in the west end of Shield's Addition. Margaret is listed in the
census records of 1800 as Margaret Gillelan, 1810 as M. Gillen,
and 1820 as Margaret Gilland.
Another form of evidence of the Gilliland family is from the
tombstones. One of the earliest tombstones of the Gilliland
family can be found at Tom's Creek Presbyterian churchyard. It
is dated 1792 and records the short life of John Gililand who
was almost five years old at the time of his death. There are
several unmarked graves surrounding this tombstone, perhaps
the final resting place of other Gilliland family members.
Nearby at Pineycreek Presbyterian churchyard near Harney is
the tombstone of Mary Gillelan. She died in 1829 at the age of
57 years. The next grave is unmarked and is most likely the
grave of her husband. Mary is interred in the Gillelan,
Correll, Crabbs family plot, of whom were her descendants.
In 1798, John Gilleland was married to Mary Hays and the
following year they were the parents of a daughter, Elizabeth
'Betsey' Gillelan. Betsey Gilland was married in 1818 to
Christian Correll. They were the parents of Lydia Correll who
married John Crabbs.
John and Mary Gillelan were probably the parents of other
children, unfortunately, at this time, no further record has
been found. John was probably the grandson of John and Hester
Rome Gilleylen. According to the Orphan's Court of 1785, Hester
Gillelan was appointed guardian of John Gillelan. In 1798 John
Gilleylan held the deed to Epping Forrest, the Gilleylen home
farm, which was previously assessed to Hester Gillylan. Epping

Forest consisted of 200 acres and was located in the Taneytown
and Piney Creek Hundred, on the Big Road leading from Taneytown
to Emmitsburg.
John is listed in the Deed Records of Frederick County from
1800 to 1833. He is also listed in the census of 1810 as J.
Gillilyn, 1820 as John Gillelan, and 1830 as John Gilleland.
He is not listed in the 1840 census and therefore it is assumed
that he died before that census.
Two more tombstones of the Gillelan family can be found at the
Baptist Cemetery, located a few miles west of Taneytown, on the
Taneytown-Emmitsburg Road. Also interred in this cemetery are
other families connected to the Gillelan family, including the
Jones, Sheeley, and Correll family members.
William R. Gillelan was a Justice of the Peace and a Constable
of Frederick County. In 1832 he was married to Ann Jones, the
daughter of Thomas Jones. William and Ann's six month old son,
John Thomas Gillelan, died on January 7, 1834, and was interred
at the Baptist Cemetery. Six months later, at the age of 28
years, William died and was interred beside his son.
A few years later, Ann the widow of William, was married in
1836 at Gettysburg, to Caleb Sheeley and resided in Frederick
County. Ann died in 1895 and was interred with other members of
her family at the Baptist Cemetery.
There are at least two landmarks in Maryland which bear the
family name. One is Gillilan's Mountain also known as Gilliland
Knob. It is located in the Clear Spring District of what was
Frederick County, but now Washington County, west of Conococheque
and north of Clear Spring. This was probably named after the
early Gilliland family which settled in the area about 1750.
Another landmark is Gillen Falls, a small branch of the South
Branch of the Patapsco River in what is now Carroll County.

JOHN GILLEYLEN 1706–1784.
John was born in 1706 in County Down, Ireland, of Welsh,
English, and Scot-Irish descent. Some of his descendants claim
descent from the three Gilliland brothers who emigrated from
Ireland to America in 1740. These brothers were descendants of
Willy Gilliland, the Scotchman who fled Scotland to Northern
Ireland in the 17th century.
Further research indicates that a Mr. Gilliland emigrated from
Ulster, Ireland and arrived at New Castle, Delaware in 1730.
With him were his children, Thomas, John, Sarah, Adam, Robert,
Hugh, James, Andrew, Jane, Mary Ann, and Catherine 'Kitty', who
remained in Ireland. Three of the brothers emigrated first and
the rest of the family followed at a latter date. They settled
in Chester County, Pennsylvania and later moved on to Maryland,
Ohio and Kentucky.
The first evidence of John in Pennsylvania is in 1740. At that
time, on April 12, 1740, James Russell, a merchant of Upper
Providence, Chester County, sold 26 acres of land for 60 pounds
to John Gilleylan, a merchant of Philadelphia.

In 1742 John was married at the First Presbyterian Church of Philadelphia to Hester Rome, the daughter of John Rome, a merchant of New York City. Their home was located on Chestnut Street and John's mercantile business was nearby on Market Street, now located in historic downtown near Independence Hall.
By 1747 John and his family had moved to Bucks County. They were members of the Dutch Reformed Church of Churchville where several of their children were baptized.
On November 20, 1751, Deborah Claypoole Coleman, widow of William Coleman, and daughter of Abraham Claypoole, late merchant of Philadelphia, sold 500 acres of land to John Gilleylen, a merchant of Philadelphia. This land was a working farm plantation located at the Brandywine Manor of East Caln Township in Chester County. It was known as the King Grier Farm and later the Benton Hanley Farm.
Here at Brandywine John continued his mercantile business and ventured into farming. At first the Gilleylen family were members of the Brandywine Presbyterian Church and later were members of the Seceder Church which was located on the Gilleylen farm.
In 1755 tragedy invaded the home of the Gilleylen family. In August John Myrack of East Caln, murdered his wife, two of his own children, and a child of John Gilliland's that was nursing at the Myrack home. Afterwards Myrack tried to escape but was captured and confined to the Chester jail. In September he was found guilty and received the sentence of death.
During the American Revolution John was a Commander of an Observation Post. Three of his sons were also Soldiers of the American Revolution. William, Peter, and Jacob Gilliland were members of the Pennsylvania Militia of Chester County. During these troubled times his son John Jr. was killed by Hessian Soldiers after the Battle of Brandywine in 1777. He was fifteen years old and was interred in the Seceder Cemetery.
From 1778 to 1780 John operated the Bull's Head Tavern in West Nanmeal Township. He is listed in the 1779 tax list as John Gulilan, tavern keeper, 100 acres, West Nantmill Township and 1780 as John Guliland, tavern keeper. In those days the taverns were a center of information and news, and tavern keeping was a highly respectable and influential calling.
By 1780 John and some of his family had moved to Frederick County, Maryland. He purchased 200 acres of Epping Forest, which was originally granted to Philip Key. It was located in the Piney Creek and Taneytown Hundred.
By the time John moved to Frederick County, three of his children had predeceased him, and two of his daughters had married and remained in Chester County. His daughter Jane was married in 1783 to James Shields and resided near Emmitsburg, and his sons Peter and Jacob lived near Taneytown. Jacob later married Agnes Shields, a sister of his brother-in-law James Shields

John died in 1784 and a coroner's inquest was held October 23, 1784, by John McAllister in Tom's Creek Hundred. According to the inquest, John Gilliand was found dead in the mill race of Jacob Hockensmith. Sixteen jurors found his death as accidental drowning. It appears that John fell from his horse and drowned in the race of Hockensmith's mill. The Hockensmith family resided a few miles east of Emmitsburg where they operated a tavern and mill.

An inventory of John's estate was appraised November 13, 1784 and proved in court February 8, 1785. His son Peter Gillelan and son-in-law James Shields were the administrators. The inventory consisted of five pages and was appraised at over 226 pounds sterling. Within this record the name is spelled Gilleylen, Gillellan, and Gillelan. The handwriting is in different styles, probably that of the appraisers and the registrar. Hester appears in this document as the nearest of kin and her signature is recorded in small letters as hester gilleylen. The accounts of John's estate was proved in court February 10, 1786 with a list of debts due to the estate of John Gilleylen and the final account was dated November 1, 1786.

In 1785 Hester Gillelan was appointed guardian of John Gillelan, heir of John Gillelan, deceased of Frederick County. From this record it appears that Hester was appointed guardian of her minor aged grandson John.

William Clingan and James Moore were appointed in a search of the estate of John Gilleylen in Chester County, Pennsylvania. On May 25, 1790 James Moore reported to the court that there was no estate to be found in Chester County.

Hester is listed in the 1790 census as Hester Gilleland with a household of 1 male under sixteen and two females. The male under sixteen was probably John Gillelan of whom Hester was appointed guardian of in 1785.

By the 1800 census she is listed as Hester Gillerlin of the Taneytown District. Her household consisted of 1 male between the age of 16 and 26, 1 female between the age of 16 and 26, 1 female under 10, and 2 females over 45. By this census Hester's family had an additional 2 females. In 1798 John Gilleland was married to Mary Hays, and the following year they became the parents of a daughter, Elizabeth 'Betsey' Gillelan. This would account for the growth in Hester's family.

Hester does not appear in the census records after 1800, so it is assumed that she died sometime between 1800 and 1810. John and Hester were members of the Presbyterian Church, and were probably interred at Tom's Creek or Piney Creek Presbyterian Cemetery. Both of these cemeteries were located near their home and other members of the Gilliland family are interred therein. There is also the possibility that they were interred on the Gilleylen home farm of Epping Forest. The early pioneer families often buried their dead in a family cemetery on the home farm.

John and Hester were the parents of 10 known children. Their child that was murdered is not listed here since there is no further information on this child.

1. William Gilleylen 1743-c1780. William Gillelan was born September 12, 1743 and baptized September 15, 1743 at the First Presbyterian Church of Philadelphia. He was a Soldier of the American Revolution and a member of the Chester County Militia and is listed as William Gilliland. Research indicates that his wife was Jane Liggett, the daughter of Ludowick and Susannah Liggett of East Caln Township in Chester County. Evidence of this is in the will of Ludowick Liggett. His will was written in 1780 and probated in 1786 and lists his deceased daughter Jane's two minor aged sons William Gillilan to receive 30 pounds plus clothing and schooling during his minority, and John Gillilan to receive 10 pounds plus clothing and schooling during his minority. They resided with their paternal grandparents John and Hester Gilleylen when they moved to Frederick County. William was most likely the eldest of the 2 sons and probably was of age in 1785 when his grandmother Hester Gillelan was appointed guardian of the youngest son John Gillelan. William and John are most likely the ancestors of the Gillelan family of Frederick County. These two names appeared in the records of Frederick County for many generations.

2. Susanna Gilleylen. Susanna was born October 3, 1744 and baptized December 2, 1744 at the First Presbyterian Church of Philadelphia. In 1763 a Susanna Gillilan, the daughter of John Gillilan, was married to William McKune of Lancaster County.

3. Esther Gilleylen 1745-1817. Esther Gillelan was born December 31, 1745 and baptized March 1, 1746 at the First Presbyterian Church of Philadelphia. She was married to David Robison, 1747-1814, of West Nantmeal Township, Chester County. Esther was buried at the Great Valley Presbyterian Cemetery. She died September 25, 1817 at the age of 72 years. Esther and David were the parents of 7 children, Rachel, Margaret, Hester, Jane, Eliza, Anne, and David.

4. Maria Gilleylen. Maria Gelien, the daughter of John Gelien and Hester Rome, was baptized August 25, 1748 at the Dutch Reformed Church at Churchville, Bucks County, Pennsylvania.

5. Jacob Gilleylen 1751-c1806. Jacob, son of John Gillilen and Hester Roome, was baptized May 29, 1751 at the Dutch Reformed Church at Churchville. Jacob Gillaleam was married in 1796 to Agnes Shields, the daughter of William and Jane Bentley Williams Shields of Emmitsburg, Maryland. Jacob would have been about 45 years old at the time of this marriage. Agnes may have been his second wife. They were the parents of 4 children, Elizabeth and William of Washington County, Tennessee, John of Aberdeen, Mississippi, and Jacob Jr., of South Carolina and later of Baltimore, Maryland, where he died.

Jacob Sr. died before 1806 and was probably interred in the Shields Family Cemetery or Tom's Creek Presbyterian Cemetery near Emmitsburg. After Jacob's death, Agnes and several of her brothers and sisters moved to Tennessee and South Carolina. Agnes was married a second time in Tennessee to Micheal Woods.

6. Peter Gilleylen. Peter Gilliland was a Soldier of the American Revolution and served in the Pennsylvania Militia of Chester County. He married Margaret and resided near Taneytown, Maryland. In 1785 and 1786 Peter Gillelan and his brother-in-law James Shields were administrators of his father's estate. He is listed in the Baltimore Newspaper in December 23, 1785 as Peter Gillylen will not pay the debts of his wife Margaret and again in May 17, 1786 as Peter Gillelen, near Taneytown, will be responsible for the debts of his wife.

7. John Gilleylen Jr. 1762-1777. During the American Revolution, John Gilliland, a young boy of 15 years, was killed near his home by Hessian Soldiers after the Battle of Brandywine. He was buried at the Seceder Cemetery of Brandywine Manor. In 1941 the Boy Pioneers of Pennsylvania erected a monument to this young lad. The inscription reads as follows:- JOHN GILLILAND / AGED 15 / SLAIN BY HESSIAN / SOLDIERS / SEPTEMBER 1777. / *-* / ERECTED BY THE BOY PIONEERS / OF PENNSYLVANIA 1941.

8. Jane Gilleylen 1764-1849. Jane was born in 1764 at Brandy-wine Manor, Chester County, Pennsylvania. In 1783 she was married to James Shields 1757-1840, the son of William and Jane Bentley Williams Shields of Frederick County, Maryland. They resided near Emmitsburg and later moved to Greene County, Tennessee where they died. They were the parents of 11 children, Hester, Jane, William, John, Mary, James, David, Samuel, Milton, Joanna, and Henry Wood Shields.

9. Rachel Gilleylen was married to Andrew Buchanan and resided at New Holland and later Wagontown, Chester County. They were the parents of 6 children, Martha, John, Andrew, James, David and Isaac. Andrew's will was written May 16, 1785 and probated July 29, 1785. He bequeathed one third of his estate to his wife Rachell, lists his six children, and signed his will as An Buchanan.

JOHN AND JANE BRIGGS GILLILAND.

John was born about 1763 in County Down, Ireland. He was one
of a large family to emigrate to America in the early 1770's.
According to family history, in which his father is recorded as
both John and Thomas, was Lord Gilliland of Belfast, County
Down, Ireland, formerly of England and a member of Parliament.
He died sometime between 1776 and 1780. His children were,
Thomas, who was married in County Down to Margaret Stodgal,
Catherine 'Kitty' Gilliland Thomson, who remained in Ireland,
John, Daniel, Adam, Robert, Hugh, James, Andrew, Jane, and Mary.
Three of these brothers emigrated first and the rest followed
shortly before the American Revolution. This family also claims
descent from Lord Gordon of Ireland. The family first settled
in Chester County, Pennsylvania, where the parents died of
yellow fever. Members of this family settled in western Pennsylvania, Maryland, Virginia, Ohio, Kentucky, and Tennessee.

As a young boy, John served in the Continental Army during the
American Revolution. For his service he received a land claim
in western Pennsylvania. During a visit to this claim John was
pursued and narrowly escaped a band of warring Indians. He
never returned to this claim and gave it to one of his brothers.

John settled in Frederick County, Maryland and was married to
Jane Briggs. They were the parents of 10 children, James Gordon,
John, Nancy, Thomas, Adam, Sarah, Robert, Jane, Hugh, and
William. John died in a mill explosion near Emmitsburg in 1826.
He was 63 years old and was probably interred at Tom's Creek
Presbyterian churchyard.

His eldest son, James Gordon, known as Gordon, assumed the
responsibility of his father's family. Gordon was a resident
of the Emmitsburg District according to the 1830 census.
Shortly thereafter he operated a mill south of Gettysburg and
was married to Margaret Lawson. By 1835, the entire family,
including his mother, brothers and sisters, had moved to Van
Wert County, Ohio.

JOHN AND JANE GILLILAND OF ADAMS COUNTY, PENNSYLVANIA.

John was born sometime between 1710 and 1725 in Ireland.
John and his wife Jane settled in Lancaster County, which later
became York County and now Adams County, Pennsylvania. John is
listed in the records of Menallen Township and his farm was
located east of present day Biglerville. He operated a mill on
Opossom Creek which was known as Gilliland's Mill and later as
Fisher's Mill. John's will was probated in 1789 and is on file
at the York County Courthouse. John and Jane were members of
'The Pines' Presbyterian Church near New Chester where they are
believed to have been buried.

Their great grandson, Captain John Joseph Fleming Gilliland
1832-1906, is the only member of this family known to have
lived in Maryland. In 1864 he was married to Annie M. Crapster,
the daughter of Abraham Crapster of Taneytown. Annie died in
1873 and was interred at Piney Creek Presbyterian churchyard

near Harney, Maryland. John was a druggist and a Captain
during the Civil War. He died in 1906 at Port Arthur, Texas,
and was interred beside his wife and infant child at Piney Creek.
    John and Jane's family has been well documented in the county
records as well as family history. The family bible recorded
several generations of their family. John and Jane were the
parents of four sons:-
1. James Gilliland was born in 1745 and was married to Hannah.
   They moved to Petersburg, Virginia and later to Tennessee.
2. Samuel Gilliland, 1747-1812. Samuel was a Soldier of the
   American Revolution and was married to Eleanor Vance. They
   resided near Biglerville and were the parents of 13 children,
   Anne, Jane, John, Samuel, Sarah, Mary, Ezekial, David, Hannah,
   Lovenia, Eliza Eleanor, Maria and Elizabeth Gilliland. Some
   of the younger children moved to Tennessee.
3. John Gilliland, 1750-1836. John was a Soldier of the American
   Revolution and was married to Hannah Micheals. They moved to
   Huntingdon County, Pennsylvania and were the parents of 11
   children, Mathew, Andrew, Robin, John, David, James, Margaret,
   William, Robert, Samuel, and Alexander.
4. William Gilliland, 1753-1831. William was married in 1777
   to Catherine Fleming, the daughter of William and Mary Kerr
   Fleming. They were the parents of 7 sons, John, Samuel, James,
   William, George, Fleming, and Joseph. William was married a
   second time in 1807 to Mary Galbraith. William was a Soldier
   of the American Revolution, and served as a Justice of the
   Peace, State Legislator and Associate Judge of Adams County.
   He resided near Gettysburg and he and his wives and sons are
   interred at Hunterstown Greater Conewago Presbyterian
   Cemetery.

THE GILLELAN FAMILY OF EMMITSBURG.

    The Gillelans of Emmitsburg were members of the Lutheran Church.
Membership in the Lutheran Church was brought about by inter-
marriage when William Gillelan married Magdelena Hockensmith.
The Hockensmith family were staunch followers of Martin Luther
beginning with the founding of Tom's Creek Lutheran congregation
in 1757.
    William and his wife Magdelena were married about 1831 and
lived on the Hockensmith property a few miles east of Emmitsburg.
William was born about 1809 and as an adult was baptized on
June 2, 1832 at the Taneytown Lutheran Church.
    He is listed in the 1840 census as William Gillan. By the 1850
census he is listed in the Emmitsburg District with his wife and
five children. William Gillelan is recorded as 41 years of age,
born in Frederick County, a farmer with a real estate valued at
$12,000.
    Members of this family were first members of the Taneytown
Lutheran Church and later the Emmitsburg Elias Lutheran Church.
Magdalena died April 1, 1874 and William died September 1, 1880.
They were interred at Emmitsburg Lutheran Cemetery.

Some of their children and grandchildren were prominent and successful merchants and farmers of the Emmitsburg District. William and Magdelena were the parents of seven children:-
1. Jacob William Gillelan, 1832-1893. Jacob was married in 1856 to Mary Ann Dotterer and were the parents of one daughter Fannie Annette Gillelan, 1867-1930. They were interred at Emmitsburg Lutheran Cemetery.
2. David Samuel Gillelan, 1834-1904. David was a merchant of Emmitsburg and was married in 1865 to Virginia Flagel. They were interred at the Emmitsburg Lutheran Cemetery. They were the parents of Charles Edgar, William Robert, Harry Morris, and Anna Virginia Gillelan.
3. Hannah Susan Gillelan, 1836-1923. She was interred at the Emmitsburg Lutheran Cemetery.
4. Mary Magdalena Gillelan was born in 1838 and was married in 1864 to Lt. J.E. Simmons of New Jersey.
5. George Thomas Gillelan, 1839-1841.
6. George L. Gillelan, 1842-1911. George was married to Ida S. Ohler. They were interred at Emmitsburg Lutheran Cemetery. They were the parents of Ruth B., Rhoda H., George Samuel, John, Joshua Thomas, Carrie Magdalena, and Lawrence Gillelan.
7. Adam Sentman Gillelan, 1846-1848.

According to a letter with the date of 1879, the Gillilands of Van Wert County, Ohio, and the Gillelans of Emmitsburg, were exchanging information on family history. In this letter William Gillelan, 1809-1880, of Emmitsburg, signed his name as Gilliland. William states that his great grandfather emigrated from Ireland to New York City and settled in Chester County, Pennsylvania. He was a father of a large family, of which the daughters remained in Chester County and the sons moved south and west.

William's grandfather moved to Taneytown, Maryland and had 2 sons William and John. William was born near Taneytown and later in life moved to Cumberland County, Pennsylvania. This William was married twice. He had 2 sons to his first marriage, one was an attorney, the other a school teacher and they both moved west. The second marriage produced a daughter and a son William, who was the author of the letter.

Unfortunately, William does not give to many first names which would clarify family relationships. If the letter is authentic, the history is very similiar to that of John and Hester Rome Gilleylen.

Many of William's descendants are interred at the Gillelan famly plot at Elias Lutheran Cemetery and Emmitsburg Mountain View Cemetery. Some of his descendants remained in the Emmitsburg area, while others moved throughout Maryland, Pennsylvania, and New Jersey.

THE GILLELAN - GILLAND FAMILY OF MOUNT SAINT MARY'S.

LINEAGE CHART
JOHN GILLELAND, m MARY ELIZABETH WILDASIN, 1810-1901.
JOHN GILLELAN - GILLAND, 1834 - 1912,
m 1856, VICTORIA SPALDING, 1838-1881.

JOHN GILLELAN - GILLAND 1834-1912.

John was born on June 2, 1834, near Emmitsburg, Maryland.
According to family history his father was John Gilleland who
died sometime between 1835 and 1840. However, at this time,
there is no evidence to support this family tradition. His
mother was Mary Elizabeth'Polly' Wildasin Gillelan Ferguson.
By 1840 Polly had married a second time to Eli Ferguson and
resided on a small farm in Friendscreek, a few miles west of
Emmitsburg.
The first reference to John is in the 1850 census of the
Emmitsburg District. He is listed as John Gilleland and was
16 years old. He resided with his step-father and mother Eli
and Mary Ferguson, and his half-brother and sisters, Eli, Sarah,
Miranda, and Mary Ferguson.
During the 1850s members of the Ferguson family converted to
Catholicism. John was 22 years old at the time of his baptism
on June 22, 1856 and is recorded as John Gillelan. Several
weeks later on August 5, 1856, John Gilelan and Victoria
Gertrude Spalding were married at Mount Saint Mary's Catholic
Church.
John and Victoria resided on the Crystal Fountain Road on the
eastern slope of Carrick's Knob of Mount Saint Mary's, a few
miles south west of Emmitsburg. They were active members of
Mount Saint Mary's and St. Anthony's Catholic Churches. Their
family is well documented in these church registers, including
the birth, baptism, marriage, death, and burial records. They
were the baptism sponsors of several children and adults.
Their name has been recorded in a variety of ways and the
church records give 15 different forms including Gilliland,
Gillelan, Gilland, Gillan, and any variation thereof.
Unfortunately John's signature has not been found, so we cannot
determine with any accuracy how he may have spelled his name.
John and his family are listed in the census records of the
Emmitsburg District from 1850 to 1900. From these records we
establish that John was born in 1834 in Maryland. His father
was born in Maryland and his mother was born in Pennsylvania.
He was literate and his household consisted of his wife,
Victoria, their children, and his father and mother-in-law,
William Sylvester and Mary Elizabeth Spalding.
Victoria died in April 1881 and was interred at Mount Saint
Mary's Catholic Cemetery. After her death John placed his
youngest children in Catholic Schools. His son George was placed
in a Catholic Home and School for Boys in Baltimore. His

daughters June and Agnes were enrolled in a Catholic Home and
School for Girls in Washington D.C. Here they received a
Catholic education and John paid for the tuition until they
became 18 years of age.

John remained in the Emmitsburg area and is listed in the 1900
census of Emmitsburg. He is recorded as John Gillelan, age 65,
widower, born July 1834 in Maryland. His daughter Agnes B.
Gillelan, age 21, was also listed in his household.

John resided with his daughter Agnes after her marriage in
1902 to Eugene Hemler. Shortly thereafter they moved to
McSherrystown and later to York, Pennsylvania. By 1910 he is
listed in the census of York as John Gillen, age 75, who was
born in Maryland.

According to his obituary from the York newspapers, John
Gilland was one of the oldest and best known residents of the
East End. He died January 29, 1912 at the age of 76 years. He
resided with his son-in-law, Eugene T. Hemler and Agnes Hemler
of Rouse Avenue. John was a member of St. Joseph's Catholic
Church. The funeral was held February 1, 1912, at St. Mary's
Catholic Church, South George Street, and interment was at St.
Mary's and St. Patrick's Catholic Cemetery. He was survived by
five children, Mrs. Agnes Hemler, Mrs. Mary Peddicord, of
Baltimore, Mrs. Annie Walker, of Carlise, George B. Gilland, of
Fairfield, and Henry Gilland, of Hagerstown, Maryland.

According to his death certificate, John Gilland, white male,
widower, was born June 2, 1835, in Frederick County, Maryland.
He died at the age of 76 years on January 29, 1912, at 960
Rouse Avenue, York, Pennsylvania. The cause of death was Apoplexy
due to Arteria Sclerosis and burial was at St. Patrick's Catholic
Cemetery. The informant was his son-in-law, Eugene T. Hemler.

John and Victoria were the parents of 10 children:-
1. Mary Elizabeth Gilland, 1857-1918, and was married to James
   O. Peddicord. They resided at Emmitsburg and Baltimore and
   later at York, Pennsylvania. They were the parents of 18
   children.
2. Francis Sylvester Gilland, 1858-1858, interred at Mount
   Saint Mary's Catholic Cemetery.
3. Ann Isabel Gilland, 1860-   , and was married to Mr.
   Walker and resided at Carlise, Pennsylvania.
4. William Thomas Gilland, 1863-1863, interred at Mount Saint
   Mary's Catholic Cemetery.
5. John Henry Gilland, 1864-1933, and was married to Rebecca
   Elizabeth Staley. He was known as Henry and resided at
   Hagerstown, Maryland and later at York, Pennsylvania.
6. Mary 'Teresa' Gilland, 1866-1893, and was married to Alonza
   Peddicord and resided near Emmitsburg.
7. Joseph Francis Gilland, 1868-1877, interred at Mount Saint
   Mary's Catholic Cemetery.

8. GEORGE BASIL GILLAND, 1871-1954, was married to IRENE 'RENA'
    SHRINER and resided near Fairfield. They were the parents
    of 6 children.
9. June F. Gilland, 1873-   , was married to Mr. Lawrence.
10. Agnes B. Gilland, 1878-1960, and was married to Eugene T.
    Hemler. They resided at Emmitsburg, McSherrystown and
    York, Pennsylvania and were the parents of 8 daughters.

GREENE

LINEAGE CHART

SIR JOHN NORTON of Northwood in Milton, England.
THOMAS NORTON alias GREENE.
ROBERT GREENE, of Bobbing, Kent County, England.
m FRANCES DARELL, daughter of THOMAS DARELL, of Scotney.
SIR THOMAS GREENE, d 1624,
m MARGARET WEBB, daughter of THOMAS WEBB.
THOMAS GREENE, emigrated to Maryland 1634, Governor of Maryland,
d 1651, m WINIFRED SEYBOURNE, d 1658.
ROBERT GREENE, 1647-c1707, m MARY BOARMAN, c1660-1716, the
daughter of CAPTAIN WILLIAM BOARMAN.
JAMES GREENE I, d 1734, m CHARITY HAGAN, d 1754.
JAMES GREENE II, d 1776, m 1727, ELIZABETH DYER.
CATHERINE GREENE, 1729-1808, m BASIL SPALDING, 1719-1791.

   Greene is a common English surname which referred to someone
who lived near a village green. It is also associated with the
spring festival. During this ceremony the leading figure
dressed in greenleaves and was referred to as the green man,
personifying the figure of spring and linking the ceremony to
ancient fertility cults.

THOMAS GREENE

   Thomas Greene was born about 1610 at Bobbing Manor, Kent County,
England. He was the son of Sir Thomas Greene and Lady Margaret
Webb.
   In 1633 Thomas became an investor in a London holding company
which promised a profit from the trade of the newly formed
colony of Maryland. Thomas was one of the gentlemen adventurers
and a passenger on the Ark and the Dove which sailed from Cowels
in November 1633 and arrived at Maryland in March of 1634.
   Shortly after his arrival, Thomas was married to Ann Gerrard
Cox, a passenger on the Ark and the Dove. They were wed in
1634 on the banks of the St. George River in the newly formed
settlement of St. Mary's. Their marriage is considered to have
been the first Christian marriage performed in Maryland.

Thomas and Anne built their home known as St. Anne's on Greene's Freehold. Their home was located in the Townland plantations about a half mile east of St. Mary's City. It was bordered by St. Mary's River and St. Andrew's Creek and St. Thomas' Lot, or The Sister's Freehold, the home of Margaret and Mary Brent. Thomas built a house and was residing here when he received the patent for Green's Freehold on October 15, 1639. St. Anne's house was reported to have been two story, with frame sides and brick gable ends, and to have been in existence until 1820. Greene did not hold this plantation long but sold it to George Binks in 1644.

The early colony needed financial support, and men with some education in the law which promised a leadership for building, planning, and executing the laws. Among these men were Thomas Greene, who was summoned by Governor Calvert and in 1639 formed a council which would later become the Council of State.

By 1640 he received a grant for 1500 acres which comprised part of Kent Island and the whole of Popley's (Poplar) Island. Thomas named this manor after his ancestral home of Bobbing Manor, Kent, England, and gave him the title of Lord of Bobbing Manor. He sold Bobbing Manor on February 8, 1650 to Thomas Hawkins of London.

In 1642 Thomas had married a second time to Millescent Browne. Little is known about Millescent and she may have been the mother of his two eldest sons Leonard and Thomas.

In 1644 the colony was in turmoil. Richard Ingle was accused of treason against the king and escaped. He returned the following year and invaded and captured St. Mary's City. At this time many of the colonist took refuge in Virginia, while Ingle and his adherents plundered and destroyed the homes and possessions of the colonist. Governor Calvert raised a force of Virginians and Marylanders in 1646 and entered St. Mary's City unresisted and reclaimed the town. Calvert offered a pardon to those who took the oath of Fidelity, with the exception of Richard Ingle and John Durford.

By 1647 Thomas had married a third time to Winifred Seybourne who had emigrated in 1638. She is believed to be the mother of his two youngest sons Robert and Francis Greene.

Governor Calvert died on June 9, 1647 and before his death had selected Margaret Brent as executrix of his estate and Thomas Greene, a council member, as his successor, the second Provincial Governor of Maryland.

During Greene's term he prevented any attempt to disturb the peace of the colony. He issued warrants prohibiting entry into the colony by the Protestant adherents and monitored the Indian troubles. In 1647 he expanded the militia due to trouble with the Nanticoe and Wicomico Indians.

On January 17, 1648, Margaret Brent, perhaps the earliest advocate of women's suffrage, demanded to have a vote in the house. This request was refused by the Court and Governor Greene denied her the right to vote.

Governor Greene's administration lasted only 14 months and on August 6, 1648 Lord Baltimore replaced Greene with the Virginian and Protestant William Stone.   Some historians view this change as an effort on Lord Baltimore's part to appease the powerful Protestant influence in Parliament.

In England the struggle between the King and the Protestant dominated Parliament ended when Charles I was executed in 1649. Parliament issued a decree making it treason to acknowledge Charles the Prince of Wales, as King of England.   At this time Thomas Greene was acting as deputy governor during Governor Stone's visit to Virginia, and proclaimed Prince Charles as King of England as did Governor Berkley of Virginia.   Governor Stone retracted the endorsement after his return to Maryland.

An Act Concerning Religion was passed by the General Assembly on April 21, 1649, granting religious liberty to all Christians proclaiming religious toleration and a Freedom of Conscience. Among the fourteen signers of this act was Thomas Greene.

Thomas remained a member of the council through 1649 and 1650 until he was discharged from all offices on August 6, 1650, for usurping authority.   This was probably a result of his earlier proclamation supporting Prince Charles as King of England.

Thomas and his family probably resided on Greene's Rest before 1644 when Greene's Freehold was sold.   In 1650 Thomas applied for 300 acres between Craney Creek and Plumb Point.   He also applied for 2500 acres at Chinomuxon Creek and 1000 acres on the north side of St. Hieroms Creek.   On April 17, 1651 he received a survey for 500 acres in St. George's Hundred.   He had purchased 100 acres of Plumb Point from Philip Land and added 400 additional acres and called it Greene's Rest.   The home plantation was located about a half mile west of St. Mary's City on the St. George's River.   It extended north to Plumb Point and inland for about a mile and a half.   The southern boundary was Craney Creek and included an island off Plumb Point now called Tippity Wichity.   In the 1800s it was resurveyed and found to contain 900 acres.

Thomas wrote his will on November 18, 1650 and was probated January 23, 1652.   His friends Henry Adams and James Langworth were the trustees and administrators of his estate.   He requested that they provide for his support during his lifetime, and the maintenence of his wife and four sons, and the distribution of his estate among his wife and sons.   Each son was to receive their share of the estate when they arrived at the age of eighteen years.   It continues to give the time in years when each son would be of age.   This gives an approximate year of birth for each of the sons.

His widow, Winifred Greene was remarried to Robert Clarke (1611 -1664), a Surveyor General of Maryland, and had two sons Robert and Thomas Clarke.   In 1654 Robert Clarke, on behalf of his wife Winifred, wife of the late Thomas Greene, deceased, and her children, demanded land entitled to Thomas Greene.   In 1648, Thomas had requested 2000 acres for transporting himself, his brother Robert, other men and servants, and land entitled to his three wives. On October 1, 1666, 2400 acres was laid out and surveyed as Green's Inheritance, near Port Tobacco, Charles County, for his three surviving sons, Leonard, Robert and Francis Greene. Winifred died before 1658 and Robert Clarke remarried Jane Cockshutt Causine.

Thomas Greene, Esquire, one of the original adventurers and a passenger on the Ark and the Dove in 1634, was one of the most prominent and influential men in public affairs until his death in 1651. He took an active part in the settlement of the Province and was active in political, social, and religious affairs of the community. He was a member of St. Mary's County Assembly, a justice of the Provincial Court, a member of the Upper House, a council member, acting governor under Governor Calvert, the second Provincial Governor of Maryland, the deputy governor under Governor Stone. During his lifetime he was a successful planter, and had held over 14,000 acres of land in St. Mary's County. As a member of the Catholic Church, he and his wives were probably interred at St. Mary's Catholic Chapel Cemetery. He was the father of four known sons and became the ancestor of many prominent descendants, some of which had moved by the 1750s into Frederick County and later throughout the United States.

Thomas was the father of four known sons:-

1. Thomas Greene II was born about 1642 at Greene's Freehold, St. Mary's City and was deceased by 1665.
2. Leonard Greene, 1644-1688. Leonard was born about 1644 probably at Greene's Freehold. He was probably named after Governor Leonard Calvert who was also his godfather. Leonard was a deputy sheriff, burger, legislator and planter. He He resided at the home plantation of Greene's Rest where he died in 1688. He also held 800 acres of Greene's Inheritance near Port Tobacco. Leonard and his wife Ann were the parents of four children, Thomas, Winifred, married Francis Wheeler, Mary, married Francis Marbury, and Margaret, married Joseph Alvey.
3. ROBERT GREENE, c1647-c1707. Robert was born about 1647 at the home plantation of Greene's Rest. Robert was a planter of Charles County and resided near Bryantown and later near Port Tobacco at the home plantation of Greene's Inheritance. He was married to MARY BOARMAN, 1660-1716, the daughter of Major William Boarman and Sarah Linley. They were the parents of eight children:-
   1. Thomas Greene, 1683-1759, m1 Sarah Boarman, m2 Tecla Shircliffe.
   2. Elizabeth Greene was married to Alexander Hamilton.
   3. Mary Greene was married to John Thompson.
   4. William Greene was born in 1694.
   5. Sarah Greene was married first to John Squires and secondly to Patrick Atee.

6. Robert Greene II who died in 1749.
7. JAMES GREENE I, who died in 1734 and was a planter of
   Charles and Prince George's Counties. He was married to
   CHARITY HAGAN, the daughter of Thomas and Mary Hagan of
   of Charles County.
8. Jane Greene Campbell.
4. Francis Greene, 1649-1707. Francis was born about 1649 at
   Green's Rest. He resided at Greene's Inheritance near Port
   Tobacco, Charles County, where he died in 1707. Francis and
   his wife Elizabeth were the parents of five children:-
   1. Leonard Greene, 1691-1733, m1 Mary Sewell, m2 Prudence
      Cooper Sanders.
   2. Verlinda Greene, 1692-1748, m Thomas Sanders.
   3. Francis Greene II, 1694-1761, m Elizabeth, the daughter of
      Benjamin Wheeler.
   4. Clare Greene was married to Jacob Clements.
   5. Giles Greene died in 1792.

ROBERT GREENE I

Robert was born about 1647 probably at the home plantation of
Greene's Rest, located about one half mile west of St. Mary's
City. He was the son of Thomas Greene and Winifred Seybourne
Greene. At the time of his birth his father was the Second
Provincial Governor of Maryland.

On February 24, 1648, Thomas Greene gave one yearling heifer to
his son Robert Greene. This appeared in the Court and Testamen-
tary Business of the Provincial Court and was signed as Tho:
Greene. Thomas did the same for his other three sons.

Robert was only four years old when his father died in 1651.
Shortly thereafter his mother Winifred married Robert Clarke.
The Clarke - Greene household included Robert, Winifred, Robert
and his brothers, Leonard, Thomas and Francis Greene, and his
two half brothers Robert and Thomas Clarke.

In 1666 Robert and his brothers Leonard and Francis Greene
were granted a 2400 acre tract called Greene's Inheritance,
which was located near Port Tobacco in Charles County. It
appears that the tract was equally divided between the three
brothers, each sharing 800 acres of the adjoining plantation.
Robert's part of Greene's Inheritance was located on the main
road to Piscataway and Rowland Road. Robert also owned a plantation near Bryantown. It was located in Zachiah Swamp on
Greene's Run and adjoined Boarman's Manor.

In 1678, William Boarman gave as a dowry, Hall's Place a plantation of 450 acres, to his daughter Sarah, the wife of Thomas
Mudd. This plantation was in Zachiah Swamp on the northern side
of Greene's Run adjoining the plantation of Robert Greene. In
1679, William Boarman gave as a dowry, George's Rest, to his
daughter Mary, the wife of Robert Greene.

Robert was married to Mary Boarman, the daughter of Major
William Boarman and his wife Sarah Linley (Sinley). Mary was
born in 1660 at Boarman's Manor of Bryantown.

Robert appears in the early provincial records of Maryland
from 1647 to 1707. He is listed in land transactions, as the
witness of business ventures, servant indentures, and witnessed
several wills, inventories and accounts. Robert's date of death
or settlement of his estate has not as yet been found. It
appears that he may have died about 1707.

Mary, widow of Robert Greene, purchased 100 acres in St. Mary's
County on September 7, 1708 from William and Barbara Guyther.
This small plantation was known as Guyther's Purchase and here
Mary resided until her death in 1716.

In 1709 Mary inherited 200 acres of Strife from Thomas Frederick of Prince George's County. Her sons Thomas and James each
inherited 100 acres of Strife and are listed as godsons of Thomas
Frederick. It appears that Mary's son James had settled in
Prince George's County and was in partnership with his godfather
Thomas Frederick. They owned several hundred acres of land known
as Aire and Strife.

Mary wrote her will on May 12, 1716 and listed therein as Mary
Green, widow of St. Mary's County. She bequeathed to her sons
Thomas and James Green the home plantation of Guyther's Purchase
as divided between them. She lists her daughters Sarah Squires,
Jane Campbell, son-in-law John Squires, and grandson Thomas
Squires, to which she bequeathed items from her personal estate.
She appointed her son James as executor of her estate. An
inventory of her estate was dated July 7, 1716 and the final
account was dated July 4, 1718. Her personal estate inventory
included household items and farm animals and was appraised at
a little over 10 pounds and the bills from her final account
was a little over 6 pounds.

Robert and Mary were the parents of eight children:-
1. Thomas Greene was born about 1683 and was married to Tecla,
   the daughter of William and Mildred Thompson Shircliffe.
   Thomas inherited part of Guyther's Purchase from his
   mother's estate in 1716.
2. Elizabeth Greene was married to Alexander Hamilton, who
   died in 1730 in Charles County.
3. Mary Greene was married to John Thompson.
4. Sarah Greene was married first to John Squires and later
   to Patrick Atee.
5. William Greene was born December 28, 1694.
6. Jane Greene Campbell.
7. JAMES GREENE I, was born about 1680 and died in 1734. James
   was a planter of Prince George's County and was married to
   Charity Hagan, the daughter of Thomas and Mary Hagan.

JAMES GREENE I

James, a planter of Prince George's County, was born about
1680 probably at the Greene plantation near the village of
Bryantown, Charles County. He was the son of Robert and Mary
Boarman Greene.

It appears that James and his godfather, Thomas Frederick were
partners in land speculation in Prince George's County. By 1694

they are both listed on the Rent Roll of Piscataway Hundred for
651 acres of land called Aire. In 1701 James and Frederick,
both of Prince George's County, purchased 600 acres, a part of
a larger tract known as Strife, for 15,000 pounds of tobacco.
Strife was located in southern Prince George's County, south of
Piscataway, on the main road from Piscataway to Port Tobacco.
The southern part bordered on the Mattawoman Creek and Swamp and
adjoined the land Aire already in their possession.
    Thomas Frederick died in 1709 and bequeathed to his godsons
James and Thomas Greene, each 100 acres of Strife and to their
mother, Mary Green, 200 acres of Strife. To his wife Mary he
bequeathed his personal estate, to pass at her death to Thomas,
Jane and Elizabeth Green.
    It appears that James purchased the entire Strife plantation
from his family members. Including Strife, Aire, he also
purchased Cowpen and held over 1200 acres of land.
    James was married to Charity Hagan, the daughter of Thomas and
Mary Hagan, who resided near Leonardtown. Charity's father,
Thomas Hagan, a planter of St. Mary's County, died in 1716. She
is listed in his will as Charity Green and received 10 shillings
from his estate.
    James wrote his will on February 14, 1728 and it was probated
February 17, 1734. He gave 200 acres, the westend of Strife to
his daughter Mary Bowlin. To his son James, 300 acres of Strife,
the home plantation where his mother Charity resided. He also
gave James his silver tumbler and six silver spoons marked J:G:
and his wearing apparel. To his son William he gave the residue
of Strife. To his son Roger he gave one half of Aire and Cowpen.
To his daughter Elizabeth Thompson he gave the other half of Aire.
To his wife Charity the home plantation during her life and land
rent and his personal estate and was named executrix of his
estate.
    Charity's will was written December 1, 1748 and was probated
October 25, 1754. She gave a total of seven slaves to her
children, Charity Gilpin, Jane Green, and Margaret Green. To
her daughter Margaret she also gave a feathered bed, furniture,
her riding horse and side sadle and a seal skin trunk. To her
grandson, James Thompson, she gave a Negro boy named Micheal, a
feathered bed, furniture, 2 cows and calves, a new chest and key.
The remainder of her estate was equally divided among her four
children James, Mary Bowlin, Elizabeth Thompson, and Ann Symson.
Her son James was appointed executor of her estate.
    James and Charity were the parents of eleven children:-
1. Charity Greene Gilpin.
2. Jane Greene.
3. Margaret Greene.
4. Mary Greene Bowling.
5. Elizabeth Greene Thompson.
6. Ann Greene Symson.
7. William Greene.
8. Roger Greene.

9. JAMES GREENE II was a planter of Prince George's County and
   resided at the Greene home plantation of Strife, which he
   inherited from his father in 1734. In 1727 he was married
   to ELIZABETH DYER, the daughter of Patrick and Comfort Barnes
   Dyer.
10. Sarah Greene.
11. Eleanor Greene.

JAMES GREENE II

James was born at the Greene home plantation of Strife, near
Piscataway, Prince George's County. He was the son of James and
Charity Hagan Greene.
   James was married July 26, 1727, at St. John's Parish, to
Elizabeth Dyer, the daughter of Patrick and Comfort Barnes Dyer.
The Dyer family had been members of the Church of England, known
as Piscataway Parish and later as St. John's Parish. At this
time this branch of the Greene family converted from the Catholic
faith to the Anglican Church.
   James inherited 300 acres, a part of Strife, the Greene home
plantation from his father's estate in 1734. He also held the
deed to other tracts totaling 200 acres. He is listed on the
1753 to 1772 Debt Book of Prince George's County, a tax list,
for Strife, Greene's Thicket, Cowpen Enlarged, Girl's Delight,
and Air.
   James was a planter of Prince George's County and on November
15, 1774 he wrote his will which was probated August 23, 1776.
He bequeathed the home plantation of Strife to his son Basil
Green. He also gave Basil a Negro girl named Nell and his desk.
To his son James he bequeathed 10 acres on Mattawoman Swamp, and
to his son Thomas Edelen Green a gun. To his wife Eleanor, he
bequeathed the land where he lived and his personal estate and
appointed her executrix of his estate. His signature appears on
the will as James Greene.
   His wife Eleanor renounced executorship of the will in favor
of her son-in-law Basil Greene. This indicates that she was the
step-mother of Basil and that James' first wife was deceased.
On May 6, 1777, Basil Greene's final account of James Greene's
estate was valued at over 220 pounds sterling and 860 pounds of
tobacco. The widow received one third of the estate and the
nine children shared the remaining two thirds, each received a
little over 14 pounds sterling.
   James and Elizabeth were the parents of nine children:-
1. CATHERINE GREENE, 1729-1808. Catherine was married to
   BASIL SPALDING, 1719-1791, the son of John Spalding of Charles
   County. In 1760 Catherine inherited the plantation of
   Edelenton from her grandmother Comfort Barnes Dyer Edelen.
   Catherine and Basil were members of the Catholic Church and
   resided near Port Tobacco, Charles County. They were the
   parents of twelve children, some of which moved to Frederick
   County.
2. Mary Greene was born in 1732.

3. Elizabeth Greene was born in 1734.
4. Charity Green was born in 1736.
5. James Greene III was born in 1738 and received 10 acres of
   land in Mattawoman Swamp from his father's estate in 1776.
6. Rebecca Greene was born in 1741.
7. Thomas Edelen Greene.
8. Basil Greene inherited the Greene home plantation of Strife
   from his father's estate in 1776.
9. John Greene.

HAGAN

LINEAGE CHART

THOMAS HAGAN   -1716, m MARY.
CHARITY HAGAN   -1754, m JAMES GREENE I, d 1734.

THOMAS HAGAN

The Hagan family is of Irish descent and were from the Province
of Ulster in Northern Ireland, orignating in County Tyrone. In
the Gaelic language the name is AhAohgain which means a descendant
of Aohagan. In some instances the name is recorded as Hagoe in
the early Maryland records.

Thomas Hagan came into Maryland in 1670 and resided in St. Mary's
County. In 1687 he witnessed the will of Dennis Hasculaw of St.
Mary's County. Thomas resided at Correck Measure near Knevets
Creek in Newtown Hundred. Later he purchased several tracts
near Bryantown, Charles County. His home plantation was known
as St. James, with the adjoining tracts of Good Intent, Clare,
Lanternam, comprising of some 1900 acres of land.

Thomas Hagan was a planter of Charles County and wrote his will
on March 29, 1714 which was probated February 21, 1716. He
divided his estate among his wife Mary, who received the home
plantation of St. James and his personal estate. The rest of
his land was divided among his sons, William, James, Thomas,
Ignatius, and his daughter Mary Baggot. To his other children,
Sarah Edelen, Charity Greene, Ann Smith, and Elizabeth Clarkson,
he gave 10 shillings each.

Thomas and Mary were the parents of a large family which resided
in the area of Bryantown and Port Tobacco.
1. William Hagan, died 1772, Charles County, Maryland. He was
   married to Eleanor Hanson. William received several tracts of
   land from his father's estate, including the home plantation
   of St. James and two tracts bought of William Boarman.
2. James Hagan died 1749, Charles County, and was married to
   Elizabeth Langworth. James received 350 acres of Good Intent
   from his father's estate.
3. Ignatius Hagan died 1765 and was first married to Rebecca
   Lowe and secondly to Magdalen. Ignatius received from his
   father's estate, 200 acres of Good Intent, 65 acres bought of
   William Boarman, and a share with his brother Thomas, of
   Correck Measure in St. Mary's County.

4. Thomas Hagan died in 1743, Charles County, and was married to
   Sarah Mudd. Thomas received from his father's estate 250
   acres of Clare, adjoining Good Intent, and a share with his
   brother Ignatius, 150 acres of Correck Measure.
5. Mary Hagan Baggott received from her father's estate 100 acres
   of Good Intent.
6. Sarah Hagan was married about 1713 to Richard Edelen (c1671-
   1760), an architect, contractor, builder, and carpenter.
   Sarah received 10 shillings from her father's estate in 1716.
7. CHARITY HAGAN received 10 shillings from her father's estate.
   Charity was married to JAMES GREENE, a planter of Prince
   George's County.
8. Ann Hagan was married to John Smith. She received 10
   shillings from her father's estate.
9. Elizabeth Hagan Clarkson received 10 shillings from her
   father's estate.

KINT

LINEAGE CHART

JACOB KINT c1780-c1850, m RACHEAL 'SALLIE' GILBERT c1786-c1855.
JOHN ABRAHAM KINT 1823-1908, m CATHERINE WETZEL 1828-1907.
SARAH CATHERINE KINT 1869-1946, m 1892, SIMON HOWARD CLINE.
NELLIE CLINE 1900-1988, m 1920, JOHN E. GILLAND, SR. 1898-1957.

At this time research indicates that the Kint family is of
German descent. Members of the Kint family appear in the Catholic
records of Conewago Chapel, near Hanover, Pennsylvania. They
also appear in the records of Mount Saint Mary's Catholic Church,
near Emmitsburg, Maryland.
     Members of the family have been listed in the early records of
York and Adams Counties and Frederick County, Maryland. The
spelling of the name is sometimes listed as Kintz and Kent, but
the majority of the time as Kint.

JACOB KINT

     Jacob was born near Emmitsburg, Frederick County, Maryland and
was married to Racheal 'Sallie' Gilbert, who was born about 1786
near Emmitsburg. They were the parents of four known children,
who were born near Emmitsburg, before they moved to Mount Hope
in Hamiltonban Township, Adams County, Pennsylvania.
     Jacob died before 1850 and Sallie died sometime after 1855.
They were interred in the old Mount Hope Cemetery near Green
Ridge and McCarnys Knob. Their graves were marked by fieldstones.
     Sallie is listed in the 1850 Census of Hamiltonban Township as
Racheal Kintz. She was 64 years old and resided with her son
John Kintz. Sallie is also listed in the baptism register of
Mount Saint Mary's Catholic Church. She was baptized as an adult
of about 60 years, on December 8, 1853 and is listed as Mrs.
Racheal Gilbert Kint.
     Jacob and Sallie were the parents of four known children:-
1. Joseph Kint, 1822-1908. Joseph was a veteran of the Civil
   War, a private of the 165 Pennsylvania Infantry. He moved to

Missouri but later returned to Mount Hope. Joseph and his
wife Susan were the parents of James V., Mary, Margaret,
Susan, Jane, Virginia, Harriet Elvira, and six children who
died young and were interred at Snyder graveyard near Mount
Hope. According to his obituary Joseph was born near Emmitsburg on January 29, 1822, and died February 2, 1908, at the
age of 85 years. He died at the home of his son-in-law,
David Shindeldecker, of Liberty Township. He was survived by
five daughters, Mrs. Peter Bigham, Mrs. Wilson Eyler, Mrs.
Emanuel Shindledecker, Mrs. David Shindledecker, and one
daughter in the west.
2. JOHN ABRAHAM KINT, 1823-1908. John was a veteran of the
Civil War and a private in the 209th Pennsylvania Infantry.
He was born February 17, 1823, near Emmitsburg. His wife,
CATHERINE WETZEL, was born October 16, 1828, near Emmitsburg,
the daughter of John Wetzel. They resided at Mount Hope and
were interred at Fairfield Union Cemetery.
3. David Kint moved to Missouri.
4. Sarah 'Sallie' Kint was married to Jacob Tressler of Fountaindale. According to her obituary, Sallie died January 18, 1905,
at Iron Springs. She was survived by her husband Jacob, and
three sons, Martin and Henry of Iron Springs, and George
Tressler of Middleburg, Pennsylvania, and two brothers John
and Joseph Kint of Mount Hope.

JOHN ABRAHAM KINT   1823-1908.

John was born February 17, 1823, near Emmitsburg, the son of
Jacob and Racheal 'Sallie' Gilbert Kint. He is listed in the
1850 Census of Hamiltonban Township as John Kintz, age 21. Also
listed in his household is his mother Racheal Kintz, age 64.
John is listed in the 1852, 1857, 1864, and 1870 Census and tax
lists as John Kint.
    John was a veteran of the Civil War and as a private in
Company G of the 209th Pennsylvania Infantry was mustered into
service at Camp Curtain, Harrisburg on September 4, 1864.
Company G recruits were from Adams County and organized at Camp
Curtain on September 16, 1864. Many of the officers and men had
served in other regiments. Immediately after its organization
it moved to the front at Bermuda Hundred, Virginia. During the
Battle at Fort Harrison, the regiment created the impression of
charging the enemy's flank. But the real charge was upon the
front and the fort was captured. During an enemy attack on
November 17, several officers and men were captured and held
prisoners until the end of the war.
    During the winter, the regiment was engaged in drill duty and
the construction of roads at Meade Station. On March 25, 1865,
they celebrated a victory at the Battle of Fort Steadman. Other
victories were Avery House and Fort Sedgwick. By the time they
arrived at Petersburg, it was already abandoned and the regiment
took charge of the army trains and moved to Nottoway Court House.
After the rebel surrender they moved to City Point and then to

Alexandria where it camped until May 31, at which time the
regiment was mustered out of service.
According to his discharge papers, John was a member of
Captain Charles F. Hincle's Company G. He was enrolled on
September 2, 1864, to serve a one year term or the duration of
the war. He was born in Frederick County, Maryland and was 38
years old at the time of his discharge. He was five feet six
inches tall, fair complexion, blue eyes, light hair, and a
laborer by occupation when he enrolled.
John was a resident of Adams County and died in 1908 at his
Mount Hope home. He was interred at Fairfield Union Cemetery
and a government stone marks his grave with the inscription of
JNO KINT, C. C 209 PA INF.
John's wife, Catherine C. Wetzel, was born October 15, 1828,
near Emmitsburg, the daughter of John Wetzel. According to
family tradition, Catherine was a cousin of Harriet Lane, the
niece of President James Buchanan, and acting first lady during
his term. Catherine's brothers and sisters lived in the Emmitsburg and Fairfield area. Her brother Jacob Wetzel was married
to Anna Elizabeth Stoops. Her brothers Joseph, David and John
resided near Emmitsburg. Her sisters Adeline Wetzel was
married to Emanuel Shriner, and Margaret Wetzel was married to
William Shindledecker.
Catherine died at her home on March 21, 1907 and was interred
at Fairfield Union Cemetery. The inscription from her tombstone
reads, Catherine Kint, Oct. 15, 1829 - Mar. 21, 1907.
John and Catherine were the parents of eight children:-
1. Margaret Alice Kint, 1854-1927.
2. Racheal Elizabeth Kint was married to John Dixon and moved
   to Martinsburg, West Virginia.
3. Julia Ann Kint, 1858-1932.
4. John Jacob Kint, 1861-1931, was married to Eliza Shover.
5. William McClellan Kint was married to Mary Talhelm.
6. Laura Virginia Kint, 1868-1951, and was married to James
   Stuart Currens.
7. SARAH 'SALLY' CATHERINE KINT, 1869-1946, and was married to
   SIMON HOWARD CLINE, 1866-1933, the son of GEORGE ADAM CLINE
   and SUSAN ELIZABETH MOORE.
8. Mary Grace Kint was married to John Mackley and moved to
   Dixon, Illinois.

KLEIN KLINE CLINE

LINEAGE CHART

JACOB KLEIN   d c 1778.
GEORGE ADAM CLINE 1746-1828, m CATHERINE.
PHILIP CLINE 1786-1874, m ELIZABETH AMBROSE 1791-1856.
GEORGE ADAM CLINE 1826-1901, m 1846, SUSAN 'ELIZABETH' MOORE.

The Kleins are of Swiss-German descent and were found in
Switzerland, Bavaria, Germany, Prussia, Netherlands, Austria,
and France. Migration to America began as early as 1657 in New
York, New Jersey and Pennsylvania.
The Bavarian Kleins were landowners and farmers and made their
living from farming. One of the many coats of arms was described
as rampant lions and roses, quartered with the motto, Facta Non
Varda - Facts Not Words. The name has been spelled as Klein,
Kline, and Cline and means small or little. It was used as a
nickname referring to the size of the bearer. Members of the
Klein family emigrated to America in large numbers. In some
instances the name was changed to Small or Little.
Members of this family settled in the Jackson and Catoctin
Districts of Frederick County. They adhered to the spelling of
Cline, although it has been recorded as Klein and Kline in the
early records. They also adhered to the German name and never
adopted the English translation of Little or Small.

JACOB KLEIN

Jacob was born in Germany and settled in the Middletown Valley
of Frederick County. There were several men with the name of
Jacob Klein that emigrated to America in the 1740s and 1750s
At this time it is not known which Jacob settled in Frederick
County and became the ancestor of the Cline family in the
Jackson and Catoctin Districts. His family was known as the
Cline's of Middle or Catoctin Creek.
By 1754 Jacob owned over 700 acres of land and in 1761 he
purchased an additional 128 acres from Micheal Creager. Some of
these transactions included a Peter Cline, who was probably his
brother. In 1774 Jacob's daughter, Elisabetha Kleinin of Middle
Creek was married to David Hoffman. Jacob Klein is listed on
the Oath of Allegiance and Fidelity to Maryland in 1777 and is
listed as Jacob Cline in the 1778 Tax List of Frederick County.
This is the last record of Jacob and it is believed that he died
about that time. By 1780 his widow, whose name in unknown, was
married to George Scheffler.
Jacob and his wife were the parents of four known children:-
1. GEORGE ADAM CLINE 1746-1828. George was born in June 1746
   and died March 14, 1828, at the age of 81 years. He died
   near Wolfville. His wife Catherine was born in October 1748
   and died October 5, 1829 at the age of 81 years. They were
   interred at the Cline family cemetery on the Cline farm.

2. Susanna Elizabetha Kleinin was born about 1750. Elisabetha
   Kleinin was married on June 5, 1774 to David Hoffman of
   Middle Creek. According to her marriage record she was the
   daughter of Jacob Klein of Middle Creek.
3. John Klein was born about 1750 and died 1828. He and his
   wife Susannah were the parents of ten children and moved to
   Shelby County, Kentucky.
4. Peter Klein was married August 27, 1780 to Anna Maria Erlebach, 1761-1788, the daughter of Henry Erlebach. Their
   marriage is recorded in the register of Frederick Lutheran
   Church and states that Peter was the step-son of George
   Scheifler and that they were from Middle Creek. Peter and
   Anna were the parents of three known children, George, Peter,
   and Catharina.

GEORGE ADAM CLINE 1746-1828.

George was born in June 1746 near Wolfsville, in the Middletown Valley of Frederick County. His name has been recorded in
any variation of George, Jorg, Adam, Ad, and his surname as
Klein, Kline, and Cline.
George owned several tracts of land in the Wolfsville area.
He held the patent for Mountain Vacancy, 75 acres dated December
5, 1792, and listed on the deed as George A. Klein. He also held
the patent for Third Time of Asking, 640 acres, dated October 9,
1799, located west of Wolfsville. He is listed on this deed as
George Adam Kline and George Adam Cline. He also owned Weaver's
Last Ranwell and Meadow Land.
George is listed in the Frederick County Census records from
1790 to 1820 and his name is recorded as George Klein and Kline.
George and his wife were members of the Middletown Zion Lutheran
Church and are listed therein as G.A. and Catharina Klein.
On October 4, 1824 George sold some of his farm to his son
Jacob for 8 dollars an acre. This sale included the tracts of
Mountain Vacancy, a part of Weaver's Last Ranwell, Meadow Land,
and Third Time of Asking. This tract of land bordered on the
land George Adam Cline had sold to his son George Cline.
George died on March 14, 1828 and was interred on his farm
near Wolfsville. His wife Catherine was born in October 1748
and died October 5, 1829 and was interred beside her husband.
It is not known how many people were interred at the Cline family
cemetery. There are three marked graves, that of George Adam
and his wife Catherine and their son George Cline.
George and Catherine were the parents of five known children:-
1. Elizabeth Klein, 1775-1862. Elizabeth was married to Jacob
   Harshman, 1765-1815, the son of Andrew and Catherine Hirsh-
   man, and had eight children. After Jacob's death Elizabeth
   was married to David Delauter, 1754-1819, the son of Jacob
   and Elizabeth Delauter, and had two sons, Elias and Peter
   Delauter.

2. John 'Jacob' Klein. He was known as Jacob and was born about
   1781 and died May 13, 1858, at the age of 77 years, during a
   typhoid fever epidemic. He was married to Joanna Protzman,
   the daughter of Jacob and Joanna Linebaugh Protzman. In 1824
   Jacob bought a part of his father's farm.
3. PHILIP CLINE SR., 1786-1874. Philip was born December 10,
   1786 and died March 13, 1874 and was interred at Ellerton's
   St. John's Lutheran Cemetery. He was married to ELIZABETH
   AMBROSE, the daughter of Henry and Sophia Weaver Ambrose.
   They resided near Ellerton and were the parents of ten
   children.
4. George Cline, 1790-1846. George bought a part of his father's
   farm which adjoined the land of his brother Jacob. George
   was interred at the Cline family cemetery. The inscription
   from his tombstone reads - Memory of George Cline who was
   born December 16, 1790, and departed this life Apr 13, 1846,
   aged 55 yrs. 3 mos. & 27 days. He lived in the state of
   matrimony 32 years and has left a wife and 10 children who
   deeply deplore his loss. George was married in 1810 to
   Elizabeth Margaret Marker, 1789-1856, the daughter of George
   and Mary Miller Marker. Elizabeth was interred at Wolfsville
   Lutheran Cemetery.
5. Magdalena Klein was married to John Maugans the son of Conrad
   Maugans.

PHILIP CLINE SR. 1786-1874.

Philip was born December 10, 1786, near Wolfsville, the son of
George Adam and Catherine Cline. He was a Democrat and one of
the well known citizens of the area. He was successful in
business as a farmer and cooper and was known for his diligence
and fine workmanship. He and his wife Elizabeth were members
of Ellerton's St. John's Lutheran Church. His home was near
Ellerton where he died on March 13, 1874. He was 87 years old
and was interred at the Cline family plot at St. John's Lutheran
Cemetery at Church Hill.

Philip's wife, Elizabeth Ambrose was born November 23, 1791,
the daughter of Henry and Sophia Weaver Ambrose. She died May 1,
1856 at the age of 64 and was interred at the Cline family plot
at St. John's Lutheran Cemetery.

Philip and Elizabeth were members of Middletown Zion Lutheran
Church. They are listed on the Communicants and Confirmation
lists. They were the baptism sponsors of several children and
some of their children were baptized at this church.

Later they became members of St. John's Lutheran Church at
Church Hill, located at the intersection of Church Hill Road and
Ward Kline Road, a few miles south of Ellerton. The cemetery is
east of the church and is enclosed by a stone wall with two
wrought iron gates.

On entering the cemetery from the main gate, the Cline family plot is located in the fourth row to the right. There are six stones of granite marble and several unmarked graves. Here are the graves of Philip and Elizabeth and four of their grandchildren. Some of the stones are weathered and are difficult to read. The inscriptions from these stones reads as follows:-

1. In memory of - PHILIP CLINE - Died March 13, 1874 (1871?) - Aged 87 years 3 mos. & - 3 days.
2. ELIZABETH - Wife of PHILIP CLINE - Born Nov 23, 1791 - Died May 1, 1856. - Aged 64 years 5 mos & - 8 days. - - - She left a husband and her ÷ Children who deeply deplore - her loss.
3. Samuel S. - Son of Samuel - & Anna Maria Cline - Died Dec 15 - 1857, Aged 2 years - 6 mos. & 5 days.
4. Mary A. - daughter of George & Elizabeth - Cline - who died - Mar - 10, 1855, Aged 5 - years 6 mos. & 29 days.
5. Cornelius son of Samuel & Anna Maria Cline died Dec 24, 1849, aged 6 mos. & 29 ds. This stone is weathered and difficult to read.
6. Josias - son of - George and Elizabeth - Cline - who died Mar 15 - 1849, Aged 1 year - 6 mos & 26 days. This stone is weathered and difficult to read.

Philip and Elizabeth were the parents of ten children:-
1. Philip Cline Jr., 1813-1885. Philip was married to Nancy Hay 1809-1888. They were interred at Ellerton St. John's Lutheran Cemetery. They were the parents of nine children, Mary, Elias, Hezekial, John Wesley, Sarah E., Amanda, Ann Rebecca, and Lawson.
2. Lewis Cline, 1815-1901. Lewis was married to Mitilda who died in 1889. They were interred at Ellerton St. John's Lutheran Cemetery.
3. Samuel Cline, 1819-1895. Samuel was married to Anna Maria. Two of their children died young and were interred at the Cline family plot at Ellerton St. John's Lutheran Cemetery. Samuel and his family moved to Fountaindale, Adams County, Pennsylvania, where they were members of the Otterbien Brethern Church. Samuel died in 1895 and Anna Maria died in 1903. They were interred at Sabillasville Otterbien United Brethern Cemetery. They were the parents of thirteen children, Mary, James W., Martha Ann, Elizabeth Margaret, Sarah Rebecca, Amanda E., Lizzie, Charles Philip, Effie Jane, Samuel S., Cornelius, Penory Ann, Lorety Ann V. Cline.
4. John Klein - Cline, 1820-1901. John was married to Rebecca, 1820-1892, and were interred at Myersville St. John's Lutheran Cemetery.
5. Elizabeth Cline, 1822-1897. Elizabeth was married to John P. Gaver and were interred at Ellerton Brethern Cemetery.

6. GEORGE ADAM CLINE, 1826-1901. George was married in 1846 to
    SUSAN 'ELIZABETH' MOORE, 1824-1887. They were interred at
    Sabillasville St. John's Reformed Cemetery. Two of their
    children Mary and Josias died young and were interred at
    Ellerton St. John's Lutheran Cemetery. Shortly before the
    Civil War George and his family moved to Fountaindale, Adams
    County, Pennsylvania. They were the parents of ten children,
    Josias, Mary, James Oliver, Amanda, Lawson Henry, Lydia Ann,
    Lauretta Virginia, Susan Elizabeth, Charlotte Missouri, and
    Simon Howard Cline.
7. Thomas Cline, 1832-1909. Thomas was married to Catherine
    Summers, who died in 1912. They were interred at Ellerton
    St. John's Lutheran Cemetery. They were the parents of
    eleven children, Sarah Ann, Charles L., Philip H., Mary Cline
    Bussard, Alice Cline Moats, John F., William H., Carrie Cline
    Drenner, Laura Cline Long, Jacob E., and Lewis A. Cline.
8. Malinda Cline, 1833-1918. Malinda was married to Henry
    Gaver, who died in 1896. They were interred at Ellerton St.
    John's Lutheran Cemetery.
9. Barbara Cline.
10. Sophia Cline.

GEORGE ADAM CLINE 1826-1901.

George was born on June 14, 1826 in the Middletown Valley near
Ellerton, the son of Philip and Elizabeth Ambrose Cline. He
resided in the Catoctin and Jackson Districts near Ellerton and
later moved to Fountaindale, Adams County, Pennsylvania. He
learned the trade of cooperage from his father and was also a
farmer.

George was married on March 7, 1846 in Frederick County to
Susan Elizabeth Moore. His wife was known as Elizabeth and was
born August 17, 1824 and died May 2, 1887 at Fountaindale. She
was interred at St. John's Reformed Cemetery, Sabillasville,
Maryland.

George is listed in the 1850 census as a resident of the
Catoctin District. He is listed as George A. Kline with a real
estate valued at $300.00, and his wife Elizabeth and daughter
Mary are listed in his household. By 1860 they resided in the
Jackson District and he and his wife are listed as George and
Elizabeth Cline.

According to family history, George and his brother Samuel moved
to the Fountaindale area shortly before the Civil War. George
and Samuel believed in the Union cause and felt that their
families would be safe across the Mason and Dixon Line in
Pennsylvania. During the retreat from Gettysburg in 1863, the
Confederate army raided George's home and farm and confiscated
whatever supplies they needed.

George settled in the small village of Fountaindale and
purchased several tracts of land and built a log cabin. His
brother Samuel lived a few miles south of Fountaindale.

By the 1870 census George and his family are listed as
residents of Hamiltonban Township.   Listed in the Cline household is George and his wife Elizabeth, and their children, James,
Lawson, Lydia, Lauretta, Susan, Charlotte, and Simon.   George is
listed in the 1880 census of Hamiltonban Township, as a farmer,
who was born in Maryland, and whose parents were born in Maryland.   Also listed in his household is his wife Elizabeth and
children, Virginia, Eliza, Missouri, and Howard.
On May 2, 1887, Elizabeth Cline died at her home in Fountaindale.   She was 62 years of age.   A few months later, on July 30,
George married a second time to Mary H. Valentine.   According to
family history, Mary deserted George, they remained married but
lived apart.
By the 1900 census George is listed as a resident of Hamiltonban Township and resided with his son Simon Howard Cline.
George died on January 1, 1901, at the age of 74 years and was
interred beside his first wife at St. John's Reformed Cemetery.
The inscription form their tombstones reads:- GEORGE A. CLINE,
died Jan. 1, 1901, Aged 74 yrs., 7 mos. & 12 ds.   ELIZABETH CLINE
died May 2, 1887, aged 62 yrs., 9 mos., & 15 ds.
George wrote his will on August 12, 1895 and listed his wife
Mary to receive one third interest in his real estate provided
that she resided with him at the time.   If not the state laws of
desertion would release her interest in his estate.   He gave the
home farm of 30 acres and a timber lot of 12 acres to his three
sons, James Oliver, Lawson H., and Simon Howard Cline.   He gave
66 acres of land to his four daughters, Amanda who married Charles
Gorely, Lydia who married J.C. Williard, Susan E. who married
Samuel Baer, and Charlotte M. who married D.C. Eyler.   He
appointed his sons Simon Howard Cline and son-in-law Samuel Baer
as executors and signed his will as George Cline.
George and Elizabeth were the parents of ten children:-
1. Josias Cline, 1847-1849. Josias died on March 15, 1849 and
   was interred at Ellerton St. John's Lutheran Cemetery at the
   Cline family plot.
2. Mary A. Cline, 1849-1855. Mary died on March 10, 1855 and
   was interred at the Cline family plot at Ellerton St. John's
   Lutheran Cemetery.
3. James Oliver Cline was born about 1851 near Ellerton. James
   moved to Cumberland, Maryland.
4. Amanda S. Cline was born about 1853 near Ellerton. She was
   married to Charles Gorely and resided at Fountaindale and
   later at Pennersville, Pennsylvania. They were the parents
   of five children, John H., Kate, George W., Susan L., and
   Joseph W. Gorely.
5. Lawson Henry Cline was born about 1855 near Ellerton. He
   was married twice, first to Miss Benshoff and secondly to
   Miss Maggie ? They moved to Johnstown, Pennsylvania.

6. Lydia Ann Cline, 1857-1944. Lydia was born September 26, 1857, at Graceham, Frederick County, Maryland. She died November 18, 1944, at Topeka, Mason County, Illinois. She was married on November 10, 1878, to James Calvin Williard, 1853-1939, the son of Isreal and Lavena Eyler Williard. They moved to Manito and later to Topeka, Illinois in 1885. They were the parents of eight children, Frank, Mollie, Emma, James Howard, Nora Williard Pidgeon, Jessie, Charles, and Edna.

7. Loretta (Lauretta) Virginia Cline, 1859-1922. She was known as Jennie and was born in September 1859 and died November 11, 1922, near Fairfield. Jennie was married to John Carson and resided at Virginia Mills. They were the parents of five children, Emma, Dora, Miriam, Charles, and Joseph Carson.

8. Susan Elizabeth Cline, 1862-1941. She was known as Lizzie and was born January 3, 1862 and died November 11, 1941, at Wilmington, Delaware. On February 15, 1883, she was married to Samuel Jackson Baer and resided near Fairfield and later moved to Wilmington, Delaware. They were the parents of four children, Maude Baer Baldwin, Mary Baer Wingate, Ida Baer Hutchinson Wyatt, and Norman Baer.

9. Charlotte Missouri Cline, 1864-1944. She was known as Missouri and was born July 17, 1864 and died December 1, 1944. She was married to the Reverend Daniel C. Eyler and resided at Fountaindale where they operated a country store. They were the parents of two sons, Roy D. Eyler and the Reverend Owen Eyler.

10. SIMON HOWARD CLINE, 1866-1933. Simon was married in 1890 to Jane 'Jennie' Finafrock, 1864-1890. She was interred at St. Mary's Catholic Cemetery, Fairfield, Pennsylvania. Simon was married a second time in 1892 to SARAH 'SALLY' CATHERINE KINT, 1869-1946, the daughter of John Abraham and Catherine Wetzel Kint. They resided at Fountaindale and were the parents of eleven children, Effie Ruth, Emma Katherine, James Josiah, Mabel Edith, Clarence Albert, Nellie Grace, Willie H., Harry Elvin, Bertha Mae, Dora Katherine, and Hazel Lucille Cline.

LINEAGE CHART

ARNOLD LIVERS, 1669-1751, m HELEN GORDON.
JACOBA CLEMENTINA LIVERS, 1717-1807, m 1742, WILLIAM ELDER II.

ARNOLD LIVERS 1669-1751   ARNAULT van LEEUWERS.

The Livers family were of French, English, and Celtic origins.
Their background has been traced to the early Counts of Flanders
which emigrated to England where a river was named after the
family.

According to family history, Arnold was born about 1669 in
Flanders of English parentage. However, some historians list
his place of birth as England, while others give his place of
birth as Holland. Arnold was raised in the household of James
Stuart II, the King of England. He was a page of the royal
household and later, as a young man, served in the military.

At the time of the fall of the Catholic Stuarts, after the
Revolution of 1688, Arnold fled England, as did the royal
family. Perhaps this was due to his close association with the
royal family and his support in the military. On June 29,
1691, a pass was issued to Mr. Arnault van Leeuwers, page of
the backstairs, to go to Harwick and Holland.

Arnold was married at the time and had two sons. For whatever
reasons, his wife and sons remained in Europe when Arnold
emigrated to America sometime in the 1690s. Since Arnold was a
supporter of King James II, and was known as a Jacobite, perhaps
his emigration was secretive and the safety of Maryland was
promising.

Arnold was among those transported to Maryland without passes
by Colonel Henry Darnall. Darnall had family connections with
the Calverts who were long time supporters and were associated
with the Stuart family for several generations.

The earliest record of Arnold in Maryland is in 1699 when he
entered into an indentured servant agreement with Colonel
Darnall. In March 1699, Arnold Lyvers agreed to serve Darnall
eight weeks of each year for the following six years. He
resided on the property of Darnall in Prince George's County.
Arnold bought this property and it became the Livers home
plantation known as Timberly. It is located three miles south
of Upper Marlboro and three miles west of the Patuxent River.
Arnold also purchased Arnold's Lott at Nottingham on the
Patuxent River.

Arnold petitioned the Assembly for Naturalization on April 27,
1704. An Act for Naturalization was granted on April 29 for
Arnold Livers, a tailor and native of Holland. On May 1, 1704,
Arnold paid the Naturalization fee of six pounds at the small
town of Annapolis.

By this time Arnold's first wife had died and he was married
a second time to Helen Gordon. They were the parents of three
children, Arnold, Jacoba Clementina, and James. Sometime after
their marriage, Helen traveled to Europe and returned to Maryland with Arnold's two sons from his first marriage.

Helen died about 1718 and was interred at the Boone Catholic
Chapel Cemetery. By 1721 Arnold had married Mary Anna Drane,
the daughter of Anthony Drane of Prince George's County. They
were the parents of five children, Robert, Anthony, Arnold, Mary,
and Racheal.

By the 1730's Arnold had purchased several tracts of land in
the Monocacy area of what would become Frederick County. Back-
land was a large tract of 5,000 acres originally patented to
John Digges in 1732 and a part was patented to Arnold Livers in
1734. This patent consisted of 1649 acres and was called Arnold's
Delight. It was located to the east of the Blue Ridge Mountains
and north of what is today Thurmont. This tract extended north
to Mount Saint Mary's near Emmitsburg. Arnold's Delight became
the second home plantation for members of the Livers family. It
was located on Owens Creek and was known as Liver's Quarters.
Arnold also purchased Duke's Woods, a 633 acre tract located near
Linganore Creek, where Libertytown was laid out in 1782. He also
purchased a 600 acre tract at Little Pipe Creek, near Westminister
which was known as Arnold's Chance.

Arnold's third wife, Mary Anna died about 1741 and was interred
at Boone's Catholic Chapel Cemetery. Arnold's fourth wife was
Helena Eleanor.

In 1745 the second home of Arnold's Delight at Monocacy was
suspected of being a home of a Catholic Chapel and the location
of arms and ammunition. A warrant was issued to the Captain of
the Militia to accompany the sheriff and search the premises in
1746 but no chapel or ammunition were found.

Arnold died in 1751 and was interred at Boone's Chapel Catholic
Cemetery. His will was written June 11, 1750 and probated August
28, 1751. He bequeathed his lands of Arnold's Delight to his
children, Anthony, Arnold, Mary, and Racheal. To his son Robert
he bequeathed the home plantation of Timberly. To his daughter
Jacoba Clementina Elder, furnishings, to his granddaughter Eliza
Elder, slaves, to granddaughter Ann Livers, 50 pounds, to
grandson Arnold Elder, Cole's Good Will, 100 acres adjoining
William Elder's plantation.

He listed his lands Duke's Woods, 500 acres in Frederick County
on Linganore, 500 acres of Arnold's Chance on Little Pipe Creek,
one lot in Nottingham, and two lots in Marlbourgh and his wife
Helena Livers. His widow Helena remarried shortly after his
death to Samuel Collard and they sold many of Arnold's land
holdings.

During his lifetime Arnold lived a full and varied life. As a
young boy he was born in Holland and was a page in the royal
household of King James II of England. Later he was a member of
the military and a supporter of the Catholic cause of the Stuart
family and a loyal Jacobite. He traveled from England to France

to Holland and emigrated to Maryland where he was a tailor and
served as an indentured servant.   He is listed in the early
records as a yoeman and later had amassed a small fortune for his
time in land holdings and other property and became a gentleman
planter.   He was an early pioneer and carved a home out of the
wilderness of Frederick County for his family and the Catholic
faith.
   Arnold and his first American wife, Helen Gordon, were the
parents of three children:-
1. Arnold Livers, S.J.   1705-1767.   Arnold, a Jesuit priest,
   entered the Society of Watten, Holland in 1724.   He attended
   The College of Liege, Flanders, where he studied Philosphy
   and Theology and graduated, ordained and was assigned to the
   missions of Maryland in 1733.   He arrived in Maryland in 1734
   and was assigned to St. Thomas Manor in Charles County.   He
   administered to the Catholics of Boone Chapel, Prince George's
   County, Conewago Chapel in Pennsylvania, and later at the
   Elder Chapel near Emmitsburg, Frederick County, at the home of
   his sister Jacoba Clementina Livers Elder.   In 1740 he was
   assigned to St. Francis Xavier in Newtown, St. Mary's County,
   where he received his final vows in 1742.   In 1754 he was
   assigned to St. Ignatius' Church, on Cross Manor, St. Inigoes,
   St. Mary's County where he remained until his death in 1767.
   He was interred at St. Inigoes Catholic Cemetery.   Father
   Livers was a great lover of horses which he breed at St.
   Inigoes, he loved poetry and cultivated and collected
   flowers.   He was a genial gentleman, cheerful, hospitable,
   amiable, and social.   The daybook of Father Livers is preserved
   at Woodstock College, Woodstock, Maryland.
2. JACOBA CLEMENTINA LIVERS, 1717-1807.   Jacoba Clementina was
   born in 1717 and was married in 1742 to William Elder.   After
   their marriage they resided near Emmitsburg.
3. James Livers, c1718-1795.   James was a tailor and married
   Mary Saunders.
   Arnold and his third wife, Mary Anna Drane, were the parents
of five children:-
1. Robert Livers, 1730-1783.   Robert was married to Elizabeth
   Hardy.   He inherited the home plantation of Timberly from
   his father in 1751.
2. Anthony Livers, 1734-1820.   Anthony was married to Mary
   Wickham and after her death to Priscilla Wickham.
3. Arnold Livers, 1737-1777.   Arnold was married in 1757 to
   Mary Ann Owings.
4. Mary Livers was born in 1739 and married in 1757 to Charles
   Boteler (Butler), Jr. and moved to Kentucky.
5. Racheal Livers, 1741-1822.   Racheal was married in 1757 to
   Soloman Hardy, the brother of Elizabeth who married Robert
   Livers.   They moved to Kentucky.

JACOBA CLEMENTINA LIVERS ELDER   1717-1807.

Jacoba Clementina was born in 1717 at the Livers home plantation of Timberly in Prince George's County. She was the only
daughter of Arnold Livers and his second wife Helen Gordon.
According to family tradition, Jacoba was named after King James
II of England, and James the Old Pretender, son of James II, and
his wife Clementina. Jacoba is the Latin form of James.

On February 1, 1743, Jacoba became the second wife of William
Elder, a widower with five small children. William was the son
of William and Elizabeth Finch Elder, who was born in 1707 and
raised at the Elder home plantation of Good Will which adjoined
the Livers home of Timberly.

William had already established his home known as Slate Ridge
near Emmitsburg. After his marriage to Jacoba, he purchased a
part of Ogle's Good Will from his father-in-law, Arnold Livers.
Here William and Jacoba built their new home and Jacoba raised
her five step-children and her own seven children. Their home
was known as Elder Station and one room was reserved as a
chapel for their family and the Catholics of the area. Sometimes
mass was celebrated by her brother the Reverend Arnold Livers.

William died in 1775 and Jacoba died in September 19, 1807.
She was 90 years old and was buried beside her husband at the
family cemetery.

SHRINER

LINEAGE CHART

PETER SHRINER   1800-1860, m SARAH   1806-1860.
BENJAMIN SHRINER   1832-1865, m 1855, MARIA ANN FLOHR   1832-1919.

The Shriner family can be traced to the small village of
Gommersheim, Germany to the year 1578. The original spelling
was Schreiner and means wood worker of cabinet maker. Several
members of the family emigrated to America in the early eight-
teenth century and settled in Lancaster County, Pennsylvania.

One of the early ancestors of this family was Hans Adam
Schreiner, 1686-1744. He was born at Gommersheim and emigrated
to America in 1729 and returned to Germany. In 1738 Hans
returned with his family and settled in Lancaster County, Pennsylvania. He died in 1744 and was interred at the Lancaster Moravian
Graveyard. Some of his descendants remained in Lancaster County
while others moved to Frederick County, Maryland.

Our search begins at Friendscreek Cemetery, located a few miles
west of Emmitsburg. The Shriner family plot is located in the
old section of this cemetery. This is the family plot of Peter
and Sarah Shriner and their children and grandchildren. There
are nine tombstones and several unmarked graves. The inscriptions from these tombstones are as follows:-

1. PETER SHRINER, Died Nov. 21, 1860, Aged 60 Years 9 M. & 30
   days.

2. In Memory of SARAH, wife of PETER SHRINER, who died July 17,
   1860, aged 51 (or 54?). This tombstone is broken.
3. BENJAMIN SHRINER, Died June 5, 1865, aged 33 Years, 1 M. &
   17 D. A bronze star also marks this grave with the inscription, VETERAN 1861-1865.
4. M.S. A small white marble stone with the inscription M.S.
   and a field stone marker, located beside the grave of
   Benjamin Shriner, marks the grave of his wife, Maria Ann
   Flohr Shriner 1832-1919.
5. Emanuel Shriner, born June 1, 1827, died April 25, 1897,
   Aged 69 yrs., 10 mos. & 24 ds.
6. Flora E., dau. of J. & L. Shriner, died Feb 18, 1883, Aged
   4 yrs. 1 m. & 27 ds.
7. Laura E., wife of Joseph F. Shriner, born Mar 18, 1861, died
   Mar 6, 1909.
8. In memory of Simon P., son of Peter Shriner, died Dec. 24,
   1842, Aged 1 yr. 2 mos & 3 ds.
9. Laura Shriner Benchoff, Sept. 22, 1870 - Nov. 22, 1935.

PETER SHRINER 1800-1860.

At this time little is known about Peter Shriner. He may have
been a descendant of the Shriner family which moved from Lancaster
County, Pennsylvania to the Taneytown area of Frederick County.
   Peter resided in the Friendscreek area of Frederick County and
later moved to Liberty Township, Adams County, Pennsylvania. In
1852 he is listed in the Tax List of Liberty Township. He died
in 1860, a few months after his wife Sarah's death. They were
interred at Friendscreek Cemetery.
   Peter and Sarah were the parents of the following children:-
1. John Shriner went to California during the gold rush of the
   1850s.
2. Emanuel Shriner, 1827-1897. Emanuel moved to California in
   the 1850s during the gold rush and later returned to Friendscreek. He was married to Adeline Wetzel, 1832-1905, the
   daughter of John Wetzel of Emmitsburg. They resided at
   Friendscreek and were interred at Friendscreek Cemetery. They
   were the parents of 11 children, Mary J., Sarah E., Peter C.,
   Joseph F., Edward C., Margaret V., John F., Angeline J., Elley,
   Laura Belle, and Emanuel C. Shriner.
3. BENJAMIN SHRINER, 1832-1865. Benjamin was a veteran of the
   Civil War and died at Campbell Hospital, Washington D.C. He
   was interred at Arlington National Cemetery. Benjamin was
   married in 1855 to Maria Ann Flohr, 1832-1919, the daughter
   of William and Susan Hafleigh Flohr of Adams County, Pennsylvania. They resided in Adams County and were the parents of
   two children, Uriah Augustus and Rena Hester Shriner Gilland.
4. Harriet Shriner.
5. Simon P. Shriner, 1841-1842.

BENJAMIN SHRINER   1832–1865.

Benjamin was born in 1832 the son of Peter and Sarah Shriner. He was married on February 13, 1855, by the Reverend George W. Aughinbaugh, a German Reformed minister, at the Emmitsburg Elias Lutheran Church, to Maria Ann Flohr. According to their marriage record from the Gettysburg newspaper on Monday March 12, 1855, Benjamin Shriner and Maria A. Flohr, both of Adams County, were married on March 13. However there is an error in the month of their marriage.

On October 18, 1858, Edward McIntire surveyed 13 acres, a part of a larger tract in Liberty Township, Adams County, for the use of Benjamin Shriner. This thirteen acre farm was located near Zora, on the northeastern slope of Raven Rock Mountain. Maria received the deed for this tract on August 23, 1869, from John and Isadore Nunemaker. She purchased this land for $260.00 and it was bordered by the land of John Nunemaker, William Brawner, and her mother, the widow Susan Hafleigh Flohr.

Benjamin was a farmer and laborer and is listed in the 1857 and 1864 Tax Lists of Liberty Township. He resided on his farm until 1865 at which time he was drafted into the army.

According to his Civil War Journal, Benjamin was drafted on February 28, 1865, as a private in the 91st Regiment of the Pennsylvania Volunteers, Company A, 3rd Brigade, of the 1st Division of the 5th Army Corps. He reported for duty on March 21st, traveling through Cashtown to the Chambersburg barricks, where on March 23rd he 'put on the blues.' From Carlise he traveled by train to Harrisburg and then to Baltimore. From Baltimore they traveled by boat to Fortress Monroe, Virginia and then to City Point on the James River.

By April 1st, his Regiment camped south of Petersburg where he heard the 'heavy fighting.' On April 2 his regiment marched 28 thousand prisoners to City Point.

In his journal he recorded that he was at City Point, Petersburg, and Curve Station, Virginia. He marched in 'stockind feet, in mud knee deep in the rain' and was without food for several days. He reports of being sick, but never states his illness, but does state that several men in his company had died of small pox. He does not report any combat on his part.

From April 26 until his last entry on May 27, he was hospitalized, first at the Fifth Corps headquarters, then to City Point, and then at Campbell Military Hospital, Washington D.C. On May 14 he recorded that Jeff Davis and his staff was captured at Irwin Mills in Georgia. His last entry on May 27 states that he was at Campbell Hospital.

A search of the Civil War records found that his account was accurate. His regiment was in Virginia, conditions were deplorable, sickness and illness rampant, more men died of sickness and illness than in combat. Even the march of 28 thousand prisoners was accurate.

Benjamin was discharged by General Order on June 2 and a few days later, on June 5, he died of meningitus at Campbell

Hospital and was interred at Arlington National Cemetery.
The Military and Pension Records give us some interesting
information as to Benjamin's character and personality. He was
a healthy blu-bodied man, steady, reserved and regular in his
habits, and strictly a temperate man. He was 5 feet 7 inches
tall, blue eyes, sandy hair and florid complexion. He was
drafted from Liberty Township and reported for duty on February
28, 1865. He was mustered out at Campbell Hospital, Washington
D.C. on June 2, and died at Campbell Hospital on June 5, 1865.
He was interred at Arlington National Cemetery, Grave 12, Range
15, Block 2, section A.

According to family history Benjamin was interred at Arlington
National Cemetery and a tombstone was erected in his memory at
the family plot. Maria appointed William C. Seabrooks as Administrator of Benjamin's estate on November 30, 1865, which was
filed on December 9, 1865. An inventory was filed January 6,
1866 and appraised at $600.00 by John Hoover and George H. Kreis.
Maria's signature appears in these records as Maria A. Shriner.

Maria Ann Flohr was born December 8, 1832, the daughter of
William and Susan Hafleigh Flohr of Liberty Township, Adams
County. She was a lifetime resident of Adams County. After
Benjamin's death she remained at the Shriner home farm where she
raised her two children. She never remarried and collected a
pension until her death on May 25, 1919. She died at the home
farm which now belonged to her daughter Rena Shriner Gilland.
She was 87 years old at the time of her death and was interred at
the Shriner family plot at Friendscreek. A fieldstone and a
marble marker with the simple inscription of M.S. marks her
grave.

Maria was a member of Emmitsburg Elias Lutheran Church. Maria
and Benjamin were the parents of two children:-

1. Uriah Augustus Shriner, 1857-1901. Uriah resided near Fairfield and was interred at Fairfield St. Mary's Catholic
   Cemetery. He was married to Jennie M. Staley and the parents
   of five children, Charles, Charles Augustus, Ada, Bessie, and
   Lawrence Shriner.

2. IRENE HESTER 'RENA' SHRINER GILLAND, 1862-1937. Rena was
   born May 1, 1862 at the Shriner home farm near Zora. She was
   married April 11, 1898, at St. James Lutheran Church, Gettysburg, to George Basil Gilland, the son of John and Victoria
   Spalding Gilland of Emmitsburg, Maryland.
   Rene was a lifetime resident of Adams County and died at
   the place of her birth on October 17, 1937. She was interred
   at Fairfield Union Cemetery. Rena and George were the parents
   of six children, Bertie Louella, Arthur Benedict, John E.,
   James Henry, Mary Elizabeth, and Charles Benjamin Gilland.

SPALDING

LINEAGE CHART

JOHN SPALDING, 1450-1521, of Farnham, Suffolk County, England.
JOHN SPALDING, 1480-1535, of Tynemouth, Suffolk County, England.
THOMAS SPALDING, 1530-1573, of Tynemouth.
AUGUSTINE SPALDING, 1560-1626, Suffolk County, England.
JOHN SPALDING, 1590-1659, of Wisset, Suffolk County, England.
THOMAS SPALDING, 1640-1713, m 1674, CATHERINE HALL.
JOHN SPALDING, 1675-1726, m MARY? FIELD.
BASIL SPALDING, 1719-1791, m CATHERINE GREENE.
HENRY SPALDING, 1747-1816, m ANN ELDER, 1746-1806.
FRANCIS W. SPALDING, 1775-1869, m 1803, ELIZABETH TRUX, 1783-1863.
WILLIAM 'SYLVESTER' SPALDING, c1805-   , m MARY ELIZABETH MARKS?
VICTORIA SPALDING, 1838-1881, m 1856, JOHN GILELAN - GILLAND.

The Spalding family is said to have originated from the tribe
of Spaldas and the French Counts of Flanders. By the sixth
century some had moved from Flanders to England and settled in
the area which became the town of Spalding, Lincolnshire County,
England. From here they moved throughout England, Scotland and
Europe.

By 1300 members of the family became active in the religious,
civic and political life of England and were elected members of
Parliament. John Spalding the Elder, of Farnham, Suffolk County,
whose will was proved in 1521 names his sons, Henry, William,
and John, and is believed to be a descendant of the Parliamen-
tarians, William, Richard, and John Spalding. John Spalding of
Tynemouth, near Bury St. Edmund, son of John of Farnham, will
was proved in 1535. Thomas Spalding of Tynemouth, son of John
of Tynemouth, whose will was proved in 1573, refers to his sons
Augustine and Robert. Augustine Spalding, son of Thomas of
Tynemouth, whose will was proved in 1626. John Spalding of
Wisset, son of Augustine, whose will was proved in 1659 and
referred to sons, Richard, John, and Thomas. Thomas Spalding,
the son of John of Wisset, was the progenitor of the family in
America.

There are several Spalding coat-of-arms one of which is a
castle surmounted on ribbon, encircled by a wreath with an
attached shield with sword, and the motto of Nobile Servitium.
Another is a bishop's mitre surmounted a shield quartered in
blue and gold.

THOMAS SPALDING 1640-1713.

Thomas arrived in Maryland in 1658 as an indentured servant of
John Shircliffe. He was born about 1640 in Suffolk County,
England, the son of John Spalding of Wisset. He was well educated
and served as a bailiff to his cousin John Shircliffe. The
English bailiff served as a steward of an estate as an adminis-
trative official. Shircliffe was a tailor, planter, and owned
a large plantation in St. Mary's County. The first evidence of
Thomas in Maryland was on June 21, 1659, when Shircliffe was

granted land for transporting Thomas into the colony.
Shircliffe's will was probated in 1663 and lists his wife Ann,
sons William and John, daughters Ann and Mary, brother-in-law
Henry Spinke, and cousin Thomas Spalding. Thomas received fifty
acres of land from Shircliffe's estate and remained in the
employ of the widow Ann until 1674.
By 1667 Thomas purchased his home plantation of St. Giles,
which consisted of 123 acres. On August 4, 1674, his wife,
Catherine, received forty-two acres which was surveyed to
Thomas as Spalding's Addition. In 1688 he purchased an additional
109 acres of William's Hermitage. These three tracts of 275
acres of adjoining land were located on McIntosh Creek, several
miles northwest of Leonardtown, St. Mary's County.
By 1674 Thomas had married Catherine Hall as attested to by
the deed of Spalding's Addition, in which she is referred to as
the wife of Thomas Spalding. This is the only reference yet
found which names Catherine as the wife of Thomas Spalding.
During the 1668 Provincial Court, Catherine Hall was assigned a
servant of John Jarboe until she arrived at the age of twenty-
two. From these records we determine that Catherine was born
about 1652, probably in England and emigrated to Maryland by
1668. Catherine was an indentured servant of John Jarboe of
St. Mary's County and served as a governess to his children.
Thomas is listed in the Prerogative Court Records from 1675
to 1698. He is listed as a Debtor in the inventory of John
Jarboe in 1675 and Edward Clarke in 1677. He received payments
from the estate of James Peane in 1680 and from Peter Miller in
1686. In 1693 he was administrator and executor of the estate
of Peter Marsham. Thomas witnessed the will of John Davis in
1690 and appeared in court in 1698 to prove the will. In 1695
his land was listed as a reference to the location of land
inherited by Henry and William Spinke, heirs of Henry Spinke.
Thomas sold Spalding's Addition in 1710 to his son William.
This is the last record of Thomas and assume that his wife was
deceased since she is not mentioned in the deed. It is believed
that Thomas died in 1713, without a will, so it is difficult to
determine the names of his children.
From an indentured servant emmigrant, to a land owner, Thomas
became a successful planter and farmer and is considered to be
one of the prominent and wealthy men of St. Mary's County. He
adhered to his Catholic faith during a time of religious
intolerance. His descendants intermarried with other prominent
families of southern Maryland and moved throughout Maryland and
the United States.
Thomas and Catherine were the parents of five known sons:-
1. JOHN SPALDING, c 1675-1726.   John was a planter of St.
Mary's and Charles Counties and his first wife was MARY?
FIELDS, the daughter of Edward Fields, of St, Mary's County.
She died before 1720 and had four children, John, William,
BASIL, and Mary. John's second wife was Priscilla Harrison
Smith and they moved to Lone Manor, near Port Tobacco, Charles
County, Maryland, where John died in 1726.

2. William Spalding, 1678-1741. William was a planter of St.
   Mary's County and was married to Susannah (Ann) Jenkins, the
   daughter of Thomas and Ann Jenkins of Charles County. William
   purchased Spalding's Addition from his father in 1710.
3. Peter Spalding died in 1741 and was married to Elizabeth.
4. Thomas Spalding II, 1688-1819. Thomas was married to Honora
   Cole, the daughter of Edward Cole. His second wife was
   Rebecca. Thomas seems to have been quite a character, long
   lived 130 years, and by the time of his will he had forgotten
   his own history. He could not remember his wives or children.
   He was aprosperous farmer and planter and the father of twenty
   children.
5. Edward Spalding, 1689-1771. Edward was married first to Ann,
   and after her death to Mary. They resided at Beaver Dam
   Manor in St. Mary's County.

JOHN SPALDING I 1675-1726.

John was born about 1675 at the home plantation of St. Giles,
the son of Thomas and Catherine Hall Spalding. He was probably
named after his grandfather, John Spalding of Wisset, England.
His first wife was the daughter of Edward Field of St. Mary's
County. It is believed that her name was Mary. John and Mary
were the parents of four children, John, William, Basil, and
Mary.

John was a planter and owned several plantations in St. Mary's
and Charles Counties. He lived on the home plantation of St.
Giles and aquired other tracts in the same area. In 1711 he
purchased the 100 acre tract of Batchelor's Rest from his
father-in-law, Edward Field. In conjunction with his brother
Thomas, they purchased 100 acres of the Tavern in 1712. By 1713
John's land speculation had moved into Charles County where he
purchased 200 acres of Green's Inheritance, near Port Tobacco.
Then in 1714 he and his brother William purchased 165 acres
which they named Two Brothers. At this time John had aquired
almost 700 acres of land.

Sometime after 1720 John had married Priscilla Smith Harrison
and moved to Lone Manor near Port Tobacco. Priscilla was the
widow of William Smith, who died in 1717, and William Harrison,
who died in 1720. John and Priscilla were the parents of Charles
Spalding.

John died in 1726 at his home near Port Tobacco. The July
Court of 1726 issued a citation against Priscilla as to why she
refused to take letters on the estate of her deceased husband.
Her petition to the September Court gives some question of the
authenticity of the will which was presented by her step-son
John Spalding. The will was read and proved to be authentic and
was probated September 14, 1726.

John's will was written January 18, 1726 and left bequests to
his wife and children including his lands of which were a part of
Calverton Manor, Lone Manor, Green's Inheritance, of Charles
County, and Batchelor's Rest, Two Brothers, part of St. Giles and
a tract in Beaver Dam Manor, in St. Mary's County. To his wife,

Priscilla, he gave the home plantation of Lone Manor and one
third share of the residue of his estate with the remaining
residue to his children. After the death of his mother, Charles
was to receive the home plantation of Lone Manor. To his son
John, 100 acres of Batchelor's Rest and his part of Two Brothers
and St. Giles. John was also appointed joint executor with
Priscilla and was in charge of the minor children's education.
To his sons William and Basil, at the age of 18, received 200
acres of Green's Inheritance, near Port Tobacco, Charles County,
and a tract on Beaver Dam Manor, in St. Mary's County. To his
daughter Mary, he gave personal estate and a share of the
residue of his estate.

The inventory of John's estate was appraised November 4, 1726,
and included the plantation in Charles County and the lower
plantation in St. Mary's County. The account of John's estate
is a five page list, including the household, farm equiptment,
animals, crops in field, one white servant, twelve Negroes, and
Cattle. The final account was dated November 12, 1727 and was
valued at 13,644 pounds of tobacco, legal tender, and over 549
pounds sterling.

John was the father of five children:-

1. John Spalding II was married to Elizabeth Brooke, the daughter
of Robert and Grace Brooke, and the widow of Cuthbert Fenwick.
John inherited Batchelor's Rest and a part of Two Brothers
and St. Giles from his father's estate. John died in 1758.

2. William Spalding was married to Elizabeth. He inherited
jointly with his brother Basil, Green's Inheritance, Charles
County, and a tract on Beavers Dam Manor in St. Mary's
County from his father's estate. William died in 1765.

3. BASIL SPALDING was born about 1719 and died September 26,
1791. He was married about 1746 to CATHERINE GREENE, 1730-
1808, the daughter of James Greene and Elizabeth Dyer Greene.
They resided at Pleasant Level, Pomfret, Charles County.
Basil inherited from his father's estate, a part of Green's
Inheritance, Charles County and a tract on Beavers Dam Manor
in St. Mary's County.

4. Mary Spalding was married to William Carter. Mary inherited
a part of her father's esate and a share of the residue of
his esate in 1726.

5. Charles Spalding inherited the home plantation of Lone Manor
in Charles County from his father's esate in 1726.

BASIL SPALDING 1719-1791.

Basil was born about 1719 at the home plantation of St. Giles
in St. Mary's County, the son of John Spalding. When he became
18 years old, he inherited from his father's estate, a part of
two tracts of land, Green's Inheritance in Charles County and
a tract on Beavers Dam Manor in St. Mary's County.

By 1747 he had married Catherine Greene, the daughter of James
Greene II and his wife Elizabeth Dyer. Catherine was born February 16, 1729 at Piscataway, Prince George's County. She was a
descendant of Thomas Greene, the immigrant and second proprietary
governor of Maryland.

In 1748 Basil purchased 350 acres of Buzzard Island and Carter's
Inheritance from William Carter. Basil had received Green's
Inheritance from his father's estate in 1726. He is listed in the
Debt Books of Charles County for Green's Inheritance for the
years 1753 thru 1774. The Debt Books were a property tax levied
by Great Britian.

In 1760 Catherine inherited the plantation of Edelenton, of
Piscataway, Prince George's County. Thomas Edelen had married
Comfort Barnes Dyer, who was the grandmother of Catherine.
Thomas died in 1749 and gave his home plantation of Edelenton
to his wife Comfort during her life, and then to his god-daughter,
Catherine Spalding. By 1775 Basil received the patent for 424
acres of Edelenton and Edelen's Addition.

Basil is listed in the 1775-1778 Census of Port Tobacco Upper
Hundred. On February 28, 1778, Basil Spalding of Charles County
signed the Oath of Fidelity during the Revolutionary War. Both
Basil and his son Basil Jr. are listed in the 1783 Assessment as
owners of property in the 4th District of Charles County. Basil
is also listed in the 1790 Census of Charles County with a
family of 2 males, 4 females and 19 slaves.

Basil died September 26, 1791 at his home near Port Tobacco.
His will was written September 12, 1791 and was probated at
LaPlata on March 5, 1792. He lists his wife and 12 children.
Among his bequests, he gave his wife Catherine, the home planta-
tion called Cold Pasture, during her lifetime, then to his
daughter Ann, Christianne, and Mary Elizabeth. His remaining
land was equally divided among his sons, Basil, Edward, and George
Hilary. As to his other children, Henry, John, William, James,
Elizabeth, and Catherine Elder, they had already received their
share. He appointed his wife Catherine and children, Ann,
Christianne, Mary Elizabeth, and George Hilary as joint executors.
He gave a total of 19 slaves to his wife and children, and his
signature is recorded as Basil Spalding.

Basil was the only son of John Spalding to remain in Charles
County. He owned several tracts of land in Charles and Prince
George's Counties. He was a successful planter and was well
known and a prominent citizen of Charles County.

Basil and Catherine were the parents of twelve children:-
1. HENRY SPALDING, 1747-1816. Henry was a Soldier of the
   American Revolution. He was married in 1771 to ANN ELDER,
   1746-1806, the daughter of William Elder and Jacoba Clementina
   Livers Elder. They resided near Taneytown, Maryland.
2. Elizabeth Spalding, 1750-1848. Elizabeth was married in 1771
   to Thomas H. Elder, 1748-1832. They resided at Harbaugh
   Valley, Frederick County and moved in 1801 to Nelson County,
   Kentucky.

3. John Spalding, 1752-1820.
4. William Spalding, 1755-1801. William was a Soldier of the American Revolution and was married in 1784 to Mary Lilly, the daughter of Richard and Mary Elder Lilly. They resided at Baltimore, Maryland.
5. Catherine Spalding, 1767-1834. Catherine was married to Francis Elder, a Soldier of the American Revolution, and a son of William and Jacoba Clementina Livers Elder.
6. Basil Spalding, 1759-1828. Basil was married in 1787 to Mary Brawner, the daughter of Richard and Elizabeth Elder Brawner. They resided in Charles County.
7. Edward Spalding, died 1808, Nelson County, Kentucky. He deserted his Maryland family, obligations and debts and moved to Kentucky. He was married to Juliet Boarman.
8. George Hilary Spalding, 1770-1820.
9. James Spalding, 1774-1852. James was married to Eleanor Gardiner and settled near Bardstown, Kentucky.
10. Ann Spalding.
11. Christianne Spalding died in 1793.
12. Mary Elizabeth Spalding was married in 1798 to Joseph Stansberry.

HENRY SPALDING I   1747-1816.

Henry was born in 1747 at the home plantation of Greene's Inheritance near Port Tobacco, Upper Port Tobacco Hundred, Charles County. He was the son of Basil and Catherine Greene Spalding.

He was married in 1771 at Edge Grove Conewago Catholic Chapel, near Hanover, Pennsylvania, to Ann Elder, the daughter of William and Jacoba Clementina Livers Elder. Ann was born in 1746 at the Elder home of Pleasant Level, near Emmitsburg.

Henry and Ann are well documented in the records of Frederick County. In 1775, Ann is listed in the will of her father, William Elder, who bequeathed to his daughter Anne Spaulding, one negro girl named Cate which she already had in her service, stock, one feathered bed and 10 pounds Pennsylvania currency.

After their marriage they resided in Port Tobacco Upper Hundred of Charles County. By 1776 they resided in St. John's and Prince George's Parish in Prince George's County. They are listed in the 1776 census as Henry, age 27, Ann, age 24, one son age 1, and one daughter age 4, and three slaves.

Henry was a Soldier of the American Revolution and enlisted in 1777 as a private in the Maryland Second Regiment. He remained in active service until his discahrge in 1780.

Henry was a testator to the will of Elizabeth Green, widow of Prince George's County in 1777. The brothers, Henry, John, James, and William Spalding of Prince George's County, signed the Oath of Fidelity to Maryland during the Revolutionary War in 1778. Henry was a grand juror in the 1778 County Court of Upper Marlboroughtown.

By 1783 Henry had moved to Frederick County and was a trustee
in the will of Richard Brawner. In 1784 he is listed as a juror
in the Frederick County Coroner's Inquest in the accidental
drowning death of John Gilliand. Henry witnessed the will of
Samuel Ferguson Sr. in 1794. He was a Frederick County commis-
sioner for the years 1801 and 1803 and a witness of Indentures
in 1801 and 1802.

Henry's family is listed in the 1790 census as 6 males, 4
females, and 1 slave. By 1810 his family is listed as 7 males,
3 females, and one free person, and 4 slaves.

His home was known as Addition to Brooke's Discovery. This
545 acre tract was located in the Taneytown and Piney Creek
Hundred District, along the Monocacy River, between Emmitsburg
and Taneytown.

Ann died on January 17, 1806 and was interred at the Taneytown
St. Joseph's Catholic Church Cemetery. Henry died on February
19, 1816, at the age of 69 years, and was interred beside his
wife Ann.

There are four tombstones in the Spalding family plot, south of
the church in the old cemetery. These are the graves of Henry
and Ann, their son John, and their granddaughter Mary Spalding.
Two of these markers are broken and in bad condition. The
inscriptions from these stones reads as follows:-

1. ... of / ... DING / ... 1816 / ... 69 years. / ... his token
   of filial / Gratitude by his children. This is believed to
   be the marker of Henry Spalding. The upper left section of
   this marker is missing.
2. + / IHS / ANN SPALDING / Wife of / Henry Spalding / died
   Jan 17, 1806 / Aged 54 Years.
3. ... + / ... HS / ... mory of / ... SPALDING / ... er 23, 1807
   / ... 28 years. This is believed to be the marker of John
   Spalding. The left side of this marker is missing.
4. In memory of / Mary R. (or P.) / daughter of George and Mary
   Spalding, / who died / Nov. 19th 1847 / In the 9th Year of
   her age.

Henry and Ann were the parents of eight children:-

1. In the 1776 census, a daughter, age 4, is listed in the
   Spalding household. She would have been born about 1772.
   However this is the only reference yet found pertaining to
   this child and perhaps she died young.
2. FRANCIS W. SPALDING, 1775-1869. In the 1776 Census, a son,
   age 1, is listed in the household of Henry and Ann Spalding
   of St. John's and Prince George's Parish in Prince George's
   County. Francis was married in 1803 at Conewago Catholic
   Chapel, near Hanover, to ELIZABETH TRUX, 1783-1863, the
   daughter of Captain Trux of Emmitsburg. They resided near
   Emmitsburg and Francis operated a lumber business. They were
   members of Mount Saint Mary's Catholic Church and were the
   parents of nine children. Francis and Elizabeth were interred
   at Mount Saint Mary's Catholic Cemetery.

3. John Spalding, 1779-1807. John died at the age of 28 years
   and was interred at the Spalding family plot at St. Joseph's
   Catholic Cemetery.
4. Basil Spalding was born in 1782 and married Mary Trux, the
   daughter of Captain Trux of Emmitsburg. Basil and Mary
   moved to Ohio.
5. Henry Spalding II, 1789-1867. Basil and his twin sister Ann
   were named after their parents. Basil was married to Elizabeth Hughes and resided at Littlestown, Adams County, Pennsylvania.
6. Ann Spalding, 1789-1869. Ann was married in 1808 to Edward B.
   Doyle and resided in Franklin County, Pennsylvania.
7. George Spalding, 1790-1854. George was married in 1820 to
   Mary Livers, 1797-1875, the daughter of Arnold and Mary
   Brawner Livers. They were interred at St. Joseph's Catholic
   Cemetery, Taneytown, Maryland.
8. Jacoba Clementina Matilda Spalding was born in 1792 and was
   married to John McCoskey and resided at Baltimore, Maryland.

FRANCIS W. SPALDING   1775-1869.

Francis was born in 1775 at St. John's and Prince George's
Parish, Prince George's County, the son of Henry and Ann Elder
Spalding. He was married December 25, 1803, at Edge Grove
Conewago Catholic Chapel, near Hanover, Pennsylvania, to Elizabeth
Trux, 1783-1863, the daughter of Captain Trux of Emmitsburg.
He was known as Frank and was a farmer and operated a saw mill
lumber business. His home was located along the Monocacy River,
on the Emmitsburg - Taneytown Road, and was known as Monocacy
Bridge. By 1850 he moved to Crystal Fountain Road, a few miles
west of Emmitsburg. The 1850 census list three generations of
the family as living in the household of Francis Spalding.
Francis was 74 years of age, and is listed as a farmer and the
operator of a saw mill. His real estate was valued at $2,000.00.
Also listed in his household was his wife, Elizabeth, his two
sons, William Sylvester and his wife Mary, and Henry and his
wife Ann, and two granddaughter Clementine and Victoria Spalding.
Francis and his family were members of Taneytown St. Joseph's
Catholic Church and later Mount Saint Mary's Catholic 'old
church on the hill.' Elizabeth Spalding died on April 29, 1863
and was interred at Mount Saint Mary's Catholic Cemetery.
Francis died in 1869 and was interred beside his wife.

Francis and Elizabeth were the parents of nine children:-
1. WILLIAM SYLVESTER SPALDING was born about 1805 at Monocacy
   Bridge. He was married to ELIZABETH MARKS? and were lifetime residents of the Emmitsburg area.
2. George Basil Spalding was married in 1839 to Mary Jane Peter-
   man at Mount St. Mary's Catholic Church.
3. Henry Spalding, 1812-1856. Henry was born about 1812 and died
   in 1856. He was never married and was interred at Mount Saint
   Mary's Catholic Cemetery.

4. Charles Nicholas Spalding, 1819-1867. Charles was married in
   1845 at Mount Saint Mary's Catholic Church to Ann E. Beall.
   He died in 1867 and was interred at Mount Saint Mary's
   Catholic Cemetery.
5. Joseph Spalding was married to Mary Ann. He died in 1853 and
   was interred at Mount Saint Mary's Catholic Cemetery.
6. Elizabeth Spalding.
7. Ann Spalding.
8. Matilda Spalding.
9. Harriet Spalding.

WILLIAM SYLVESTER SPALDING.

William Sylvester was born about 1805 at the Spalding home
near Monocacy Bridge in the Taneytown District of Frederick
County. He was the edlest son of Francis and Elizabeth Trux
Spalding. He was known as Sylvester, but has been recorded by
both names of William and Sylvester.

According to family history his wife was Mary Elizabeth Marks,
but as yet nothing has been found to confirm her maiden name.
She has been recorded as both Mary and Elizabeth.

The first record of Sylvester is in 1834 when letters were
listed for him at the Taneytown Post Office. He probably was
employed by his father at the saw mill lumber yard and his
occupation has been listed as a carpenter. It appears that
Sylvester never owned a home or property for he is listed either
in his father's or son-in-law's households.

According to the 1850 and 1860 census records William Sylvester
and his wife Mary resided with his father Francis. The 1868
Census of Mount Saint Mary's Parish and the 1870 census list
William Sylvester and his wife as residing with their son-in-law
and daughter, John and Victoria Gilliland. By the 1880 census
they are listed as father and mother-in-law and resided with
John Gillelan. The last record of Sylvester and Mary is the
1881 census of Mount Saint Mary's Parish. They are listed in
the household of their son-in-law, John Gillen.

Sylvester and Mary were probably interred at Mount Saint Mary's,
now known as St. Anthony's Catholic Cemetery, since they were
members of this church. However no record of their death or
burial has been found.

They were the parents of one known daughter, Victoria Gertrude
Spalding. Victoria was married to John Gillelan - Gilland.

VICTORIA GERTRUDE SPALDING GILLAND 1838-1881.

Victoria was born in 1838 the daughter of William Sylvester and
Mary Elizabeth Marks Spalding. She was a member of Mount Saint
Mary's Catholic Church and received her first communion on April
21, 1850 and was confirmed May 9th, 1850. On August 5th, 1856,
Victoria Gertrude Spalding and John Gilelan were married by the
Reverend H.S. McMurdie at Mount Saint Mary's Catholic 'old
church on the hill.' Their marriage was witnessed by Samuel
McCrea and Miranda Ferguson, who was John Gilelan's half sister.

John and Victoria were the parents of ten children. Their
children were baptized at Mount Saint Mary's Catholic Church,
except for Ann, who was born September 12, 1860, and was baptized
October 7th 1860, at the home of the great grandfather Francis
Spalding. John and Victoria resided at the Gilland home on the
Crystal Fountain Road, a few miles west of Emmitsburg.
    The only reference to Victoria's death is from the church
announcement of April 3, 1881, which states:- Your prayers are
requested for Mrs. Gillan, who is at the point of death. She
was interred at St. Anthony's Catholic Cemetery.
    John remained in the Emmitsburg area until 1903 at which time
he moved to McSherrystown and later to York, Pennsylvania, where
he died in 1912. He was interred at the York Catholic Cemetery.

WILDASIN

LINEAGE CHART

JOHANNES WILTENSINN - WILDASIN, 1691-1754, m CATHERINE, dc 1769.
JOHN 'JACOB' WILDASIN I, 1747-1814, m CATHERINE MOTTER?
JOHN 'JACOB' WILDASIN II, 1770-1822, m ELIZABETH 'BETSY' CARBAUGH.
MARY ELIZABETH 'POLLY' WILDASIN GILLELAN FERGUSON, 1810-1901.

    The name is of German origin from the Palatinate area of
Germany. It was originally spelled Wiltensinn as it appeared on
the ship passenger list of the emigrant Johannes Wiltensinn. It
simply means vension, from the Latin venari, which means to hunt.
The family coat of arms is quartered, with two rampant lions
with a crown upon their heads and two men. This suggests that
the early Wildasins were probably the hunters for the royal
family. Over the years the name was spelled various ways, the
most common usage of Wildasin, as well as Wildesin, Wilderson,
Willison, Wilkinson, and others of less usage.

JOHANNES WILTENSINN - WILDASIN 1691-1754.

    Johannes was born in 1691 in the old Duchy of Hess, Germany and
came to America on February 7, 1739. He was on board the ship
Jamica Galley and his name appears on the ship passenger list as
Johannes Wiltnesinn. He was 48 years of age at the time of his
arrival at Philadelphia. He was accompanied by his wife
Catherine and their nine year old son Samuel. According to
family history, Johannes was also accompanied by two of his
brothers, one of which settled in Maryland, and the other settled
in western York County, Pennsylvania.
    Late in the fall of 1739 Johannes and his family settled in the
Lake Marburg area of Manheim Township, York County, Pennsylvania.
This area is located about six miles east of the present town
of Hanover, with the landmarks of Wildasin's Meeting House and
Wildasin's Graveyard as evidence of the Wildasin family in the
area.
    Johannes and his family were among the early settlers of the
Hanover area. The exact date of Johannes and Catherine's deaths
and the place of their burial remains unknown. Perhaps they were

interred on the Wildasin family farm, as was the custom at the
time. It is believed that Johannes died about 1754 and his
widow remained in the area and purchased several tracts of land
until her death in the late 1760's. In 1764 a warrant for 165
acres called Meadow Land was received by Samuel Wildesine in the
right of his mother Catherine Wildesine. It was surveyed in 1766
and was located along Cadorus Creek. Adjoining Meadow Land was
a 163 acre tract surveyed in 1766 to Samuel Wildesine for his
brother George Charles Wildesine.

   Johannes and Catherine were the parents of four known children.
The younger children's baptisms were recorded in both Sherman's
Lutheran and Reformed Church of West Manheim Township and St.
Matthew's Lutheran Church at Hanover.
1. Samuel Wildasin, 1730-1804. Samuel was born in Germany and
   was nine years old when his family emigrated to America. He
   and his two wives, Susannah and Magdalena (Margaret?) were
   the parents of twelve children.
2. George Charles Wildasin was born January 6, 1740 and baptized
   May 29, 1740, the son of Johannes Wildensinn of Conewago. He
   died shortly after his marriage.
3. Catherine Barbara Wildasin Milhimes. Catherine Barbara
   Wildensin was born August 28, 1743 and baptized in 1743,
   the daughter of John Wildensin. The witnesses of her baptism
   were Daniel and his wife Catherine Barbara Barnitz.
4. JOHN 'JACOB' WILDASIN I, 1747-1814. John Jacob Wildensin was
   born April 8, 1747 and baptized April 27, 1747, the son of
   John Wildensin. Hans Jacob Scherer was the witness of his
   baptism. He was a lifetime resident of the Hanover area. He
   and his wife Catherine were the parents of twelve children.

JOHN 'JACOB' WILDASIN I   1747-1814.

   John Jacob Wildensin was born April 8, 1747 and baptized April
27, 1747, the son of John Wildensin. Hans Jacob Scherer was the
witness of his baptism. His baptism was recorded in both Sherman's
Lutheran and Reformed Church of West Manheim Township and St.
Matthew's Lutheran Church of Hanover.

   He was known as Jacob and was recorded in the 1783 tax list
and the census records of 1790 and 1800 as Jacob Wildasin of
Manheim Township. Jacob and his brother Samuel were members of
the York County Militia during the American Revolution.

   Jacob was a lifelong resident of the Manheim Township area of
York County. He died in 1814 and his will was probated on
September 7, 1814, but the date of his death and place of burial
are unknown.

   According to family history, Jacob's wife was Catherine Motter,
but no evidence has been found to support this claim. There was
a George Motter who lived in the Hanover area and some of his
descendants were intermarried with the Wildasin family.

Jacob and Catherine were the parents of twelve children:-
1. JOHN 'JACOB' WILDASIN II, 1770-1822. Jacob was married
   three times, first to Julianna Becker, second to ELIZABETH
   'BETSY' CARBAUGH, and third to Mary Tressler. Jacob and his
   wives were the parents of eleven children. Jacob resided
   near Hanover, Pennsylvania and later at Arendtsville.
2. Charles Wildasin was born in 1773 and married Christina and
   moved to Ohio.
3. Samuel Wildasin, 1785-1805. Samuel was married to Anna Mary
   and died shortly after his marriage.
4. Martin Wildasin was born in 1790 and was a veteran of the
   War of 1812. He was married to Susanna Elizabeth and moved
   to Ohio.
5. Magdalena Wildasin.
6. Christina Wildasin was married to Frederick Eppley and
   resided near Jefferson, Pennsylvania.
7. Julianna Wildasin was married to Henry Dewalt.
8. Eve Wildasin was married to John Dubbs, Jacob Smith and
   possibly to Samuel Lawson.
9. Judith Wildasin Reisinger, 1775-1829.
According to family history Jacob and Catherine were the parents
of three more daughters whose names are unknown.

JOHN 'JACOB' WILDASIN II   1770-1822.

John Jacob was born in 1770 near Hanover, the son of John Jacob
and Catherine Wildasin. He was known as Jacob and was married
three times and had eleven children. His first wife was
Julianna Becker and they were the parents of four children, John,
Susanna, Eva, and Jacob III.

Early in the 1880s, after Julianna's death, Jacob and his
children moved from the Hanover area to the South Mountain area
near Arendtsville, Franklin Township, Adams County, Pennsylvania.
While residing in Adams County, Jacob bought two tracts of land,
one from David Boyer and another from Sarah Kellenberg.

His second wife was Elizabeth 'Betsy' Carbaugh, the daughter
of Christian and Susanna Carbaugh of the Arendtsville area.
Jacob and Betsy were the parents of four children, Samuel, Peter,
Mary Elizabeth, known as Polly, and Lydia. After Betsy's death,
Jacob was married to Mary Tressler and had a son George and two
daughters whose names are unknown.

Jacob died in 1822 and on April 8, 1822, David Deardorff of
Franklin Township was appointed guardian of the minor children
of Jacob Wildasin, deceased, who were under the age of 14 years.
Their names were Samuel, Polly, and Peter. There was a sheriff's
sale of Jacob's estate as recorded in the Gettysburg Centinel
newspaper dated July 9, 1823. Jacob and his second wife Betsy
were interred at the Lutheran and Reformed Cemetery in Arendtsville.

MARY ELIZABETH 'POLLY' WILDASIN GILLELAN FERGUSON 1810-1901.

Mary was born February 26, 1810, at South Mountain, near
Arendtsville, the daughter of John Jacob Wildasin and his
second wife Elizabeth 'Betsy' Carbaugh. She was known as Polly
and both of her parents died when she was quite young. She
received an inheritance from her grandfather, Christian Carbaugh's
estate, which was placed in trust for her use. After the death
of her father in 1822, Polly was placed in the guardianship of
David Deardorff of Franklin Township.

Little is known about her early life and first marriage.
According to family history her first husband was John Gillelan
and they resided near Emmitsburg, Frederick County, Maryland.
There is a John Gilleland - Gillilyn - Gillelan listed in the
census records of Frederick County from 1810 to 1830. He is not
listed in the 1840 census which indicates that he died before
that time. To this marriage Polly had one son, John Gillelan -
Gilland, who was born June 22, 1834, near Emmitsburg.

By 1840 Polly was married to Eli Ferguson, who was born in 1820,
the son of Hugh Ferguson. They resided on a small farm in
Friendscreek on the western slope of Carrick's Knob, a few miles
west of Emmitsburg. According to the 1850 census, the Ferguson
family resided in the Emmitsburg District of Frederick County.
They are listed as Eli and Mary, both age 33, with their children,
Maranda, Eli and Mary Ferguson. Also listed was John Gilleland,
age 16, Polly's son to her first marriage.

Eli has been recorded as Levi in some instances. One such case
is that of his obituary which appeared in the Emmitsburg
Chronicle on Friday April 20, 1900. According to his obituary,
Mr. Levi Ferguson, 80 years, formerly of this district, died on
April 17, 1900, at the residence of his son-in-law Mr. Sanford
Seiss, near Monterey, Pennsylvania.

By the 1900 census, Polly is listed in the household of her
daughter and son-in-law, Sally and Sanford Sease. She is recorded
as Mary Fargason, mother-in-law, born 1815, age 85, widow.
According to her obituary which appeared in the Emmitsburg
Chronicle on Friday September 27, 1901, Mrs. Mary E. Ferguson,
age 91, widow of the late Eli Ferguson, died on September 23,
1901, at her residence on the mountain, west of Emmitsburg.
Funeral services were held at St. Anthony's Catholic Church.

According to her death certificate, Mary E. Furguson, white
female, housewife, widow, was the daughter of Jacob Willison,
and a native of Pennsylvania. She died at Friendscreek on
September 23, 1901, at the age of 91 years.

The death records of M.S. Shuff, undertaker of Emmitsburg,
list Eli Forgason, died April 15, 1900, age 80, and Mrs. Eli
Forgason, died September 22, 1901, age 86 years. Their burial
was at the College Cemetery.

From these records a contradiction in Mary's age of five years exists which gives her year of birth as 1810 or 1815. Mary and Eli were interred at St. Anthony's Catholic Shrine Cemetery. Over the years this cemetery has been known as Mount Saint Mary's, the mountain cemetery, the college cemetery, and more recently as Saint Anthony's.

It is interesting to note that members of the Ferguson family converted to Catholicism. This may have been because of the strong influence of the Catholic Church in the area. It is also believed that the Ferguson family were close friends of the Spalding family, which had been of the Catholic faith for many generations. This may also have contributed to the change in faith. Whatever the reason, the Ferguson family became members of Mount Saint Mary's and later Saint Anthony's Catholic Churches.

According to the parish register of Mount Saint Mary's Church, Polly, Emeline, Sarah Frances, Mary Elizabeth, and Maranda were baptised in 1855. Polly is listed as an adult receiving baptism on October 11, 1855, in her maiden name of Mary Wilderson, and her date of birth is recorded as February 26, 1816. She is also listed as Mrs. Ferguson, the baptism sponsor of her son, John Gillelan, who was bapti ed on June 22, 1856, and his date of birth is recorded as July 1834. Several weeks later, John Gilelan was married at Mount Saint Mary's on August 5, 1856, to Victoria Gertrude Spalding.

Mary Elizabeth 'Polly' and her second husband Eli Ferguson were the parents of six children:-
1. Maranda Elizabeth Ferguson, 1840-1866.
2. Eli Ferguson Jr. was born about 1842 and died before the 1860 census.
3. Sarah Frances Ferguson, 1845-1918. She was married to Sanford E. Sease.
4. Mary Elizabeth Ferguson was married to David Turner.
5. Emeline Ferguson, 1852-1936. Emeline was married to John A. Hardman.
6. Ananias Ferguson, 1853-1934. Ananias was married to Carrie Helen Miller.

JOHN E. GILLAND, JR.

AHNENTAFEL CHART

1. John E. Gilland, Jr.; born December 11, 1932, Zora, Adams
   County, PA; married Emma Marie Bishop, June 7, 1952,
   Emmitsburg, MD
2. John E. Gilland, Sr.; b 1899, Zora, PA; died 1957, Zora, PA;
   married 1920, Hagerstown, MD
3. Nellie Grace Cline; born 1900, Fountaindale, Adams County,
   PA; died 1988, Gettysburg, PA
4. George Basil Gilland; born 1871, Emmitsburg, MD; died 1954,
   Gettysburg, PA; married 1898, Gettysburg, PA
5. Irene 'Rena' Shriner; born 1862, Zora, Adams County, PA;
   died 1937, Zora, PA
6. Simon Howard Cline; born 1866, Fountaindale, PA; died 1933,
   Fountaindale, PA; married 1892, Fountaindale, PA
7. Sarah 'Sally' Catherine Kint; born 1869, Mt. Hope, PA; died
   1946, Fountaindale, PA
8. John Gillelan - Gilland; born 1834, Emmitsburg, MD; died
   1912, York, PA; married 1856, Emmitsburg, MD
9. Victoria Gertrude Spalding; born 1838, Emmitsburg, MD; died
   1881, Emmitsburg, MD
10. Benjamin Shriner; born 1832, Adams County, PA; died 1865,
    Washington D.C.; married 1858, Emmitsburg, MD
11. Mariah Ann Flohr; born 1832, Adams County, PA; died 1919,
    Zora, PA.
12. George Adam Cline; born 1826, Ellerton, Frederick County,
    MD; died 1901, Fountaindale, PA; married 1846, Frederick
    County, MD
13. Susan Elizabeth Moore; born 1824, Frederick County, MD;
    died 1887, Fountaindale, PA
14. John Abraham Kint; born 1823, Emmitsburg, MD; died 1908,
    Mt. Hope, PA; married
15. Catherine Wetzel; born 1828, Emmitsburg, MD; died 1907,
    Mt. Hope, PA
16. John Gillelan
17. Mary Elizabeth 'Polly' Wildasin Gillelan Ferguson; born
    1810, Arendtsville, PA; died 1901, Emmitsburg, MD
18. William Sylvester Spalding; born 1805, Emmitsburg, MD;
    died Emmitsburg, MD; married Emmitsburg, MD
19. Mary Elizabeth Marks(?); born 1808, Emmitsburg, MD
20. Peter Shriner; born 1800, Frederick County, MD; died 1860,
    Adams County, PA; married
21. Sarah; born 1806, Frederick County, MD; died 1860, Adams
    County, PA.
22. William Flohr; born 1798, Arendtsville, PA; died 1854,
    Fountaindale, PA; married 1824, Adams County, PA
23. Susan Hafleigh; born 1800, Adams County, PA; died 1894,
    Fountaindale, PA.

24. Philip Cline; born 1786, Frederick County, MD; died 1874,
    Ellerton, MD; married
25. Elizabeth Ambrose; born 1791, Frederick County, MD; died
    1856, Ellerton, MD
28. Jacob Kint; born about 1780, Frederick County, MD; died
    1850, Mt. Hope, PA; married about 1820, Emmitsburg, MD
29. Racheal 'Sally' Gilbert; born about 1786, Frederick County,
    MD; died about 1855, Mt. Hope, PA
30. John Wetzel
34. John 'Jacob' Wildasin; born 1770, Hanover, PA; died 1822,
    Arendtsville, PA; married
35. Elizabeth 'Betsy' Carbaugh
36. Francis W. Spalding; born 1775, Prince George's County, MD;
    died 1869, Emmitsburg, MD; married 1803, Conewago Catholic
    Chapel
37. Elizabeth Trux; born 1783; died 1863, Emmitsburg, MD
44. Leonard Flohr II; born 1773, Dover, York County, PA; died
    1840, Fountaindale, PA; married
45. Racheal Smith; born 1778; died 1850, Fountaindale, PA
46. Jacob Hafleigh
48. George Adam Kline - Cline; born 1746, near Wolfsville, MD;
    died 1828, Wolfsville, MD; married
49. Catherine Weber - Weaver; born 1748, Wolfsville, MD; died
    1829, Wolfsville, MD
50. Henry Ambrose; born 1763, Monocacy, Frederick County, MD;
    died 1845, Ellerton, MD; married
51. Sophia Weaver; born 1769, Frederick County, MD; died 1841,
    Ellerton, MD
68. John 'Jacob' Wildasin I; born 1747, near Hanover, PA; died
    1814, near Hanover, PA; married
69. Catherine Motter - Matter(?)
70. Christian Carbaugh; died 1813, Arendtsville, PA; married
71. Susannah
72. Henry Spalding; born 1747, Charles County, MD; died 1816,
    Taneytown, Frederick County, MD; married 1771, Conewago
    Catholic Chapel
73. Anne Elder; born 1746, Emmitsburg, MD; died 1806, Taneytown,
    Frederick County, MD
88. Leonard Flohr I; born 1750, Dover, York County, PA; died
    1820, Columbia County, Ohio; married about 1770, Dover, PA
89. Anna Margareta; born 1750, York County, PA; died 1804,
    Arendtsville, PA
96. Jacob Klein - Kline - Cline; born Germany; died about 1778,
    Catoctin District, Frederick County, MD
98. Philip Weber - Weaver; born about 1716, Germany; died
    Frederick County, MD

100. John 'Philip' Ambrose; born 1734, Lancaster County, PA;
     died 1776, Thurmont, MD; married
101. Eva Catherine
102. George F. Weaver - Weber; born about 1738, Germany; died
     1802, Frederick County, MD; married about 1768
103. Eve Catherine; born about 1745
136. Johannes Wiltensinn - Wildasin; born 1691, Old Duchy of
     Hess, Germany; emigrated 1739; died 1754, near Hanover,
     York County, PA; married
137. Catherine; born about 1695, Germany; died about 1769, York
     County, PA
144. Basil Spalding; born 1719, St. Mary's County, MD; died 1791,
     Port Tobacco, Charles County, MD; married about 1746
145. Catherine Greene; born 1729, Prince George's County, MD;
     died 1808, Port Tobacco, Charles County, MD
146. William Elder II; born 1707, Prince George's County, MD;
     died 1775, Emmitsburg, MD; married 1742
147. Jacoba Clementina Livers; born 1717, Prince George's County,
     MD; died 1807, Emmitsburg, MD
176. John Valentine Flohr; born 1726, Germany; died 1804, Dover,
     York County, PA; married 1746, Dover, PA
177. Elizabeth Zimmerman; born 1724, Gallberg, near Heidelberg,
     Germany; died 1775, Dover, York County, PA
200. Mattias Ambrose; born 1696, Germany; died 1784, Monocacy,
     Frederick County, MD; emigrated 1732 to Philadelphia, PA;
     married 1733, Lancaster County, PA
201. Catherine Spongh; born 1711, Germany; died 1807, Monocacy,
     Frederick County, MD
288. John Spalding; born about 1675, St. Giles, St. Mary's
     County, MD; died 1726, Port Tobacco, Charles County, MD;
     married first
289. Mary(?) Fields; died 1720, St. Mary's County, MD
290. James Greene II; born Piscataway, Prince George's County,
     MD; died 1776, Piscataway, MD; married 1727, Piscataway, MD
291. Elizabeth Dyer; born 1711, Piscataway, MD
292. William Elder I; born Lancashire, England; died 1714, Cal-
     vert County, MD; married 1705, Prince George's County, MD
293. Elizabeth Finch; born about 1687, Calvert County, MD; died
     1729, Prince George's County, MD; married second Solomon
     Stimton; married third Peter Hoggins
294. Arnold Livers; born about 1669, Flanders; died 1751, Prince
     George's County, MD
295. Helen Gordon; died 1718, Prince George's County, MD
354. George Zimmerman, of Gallberg, near Heidelberg, Germany;
     emigrated 1746 to Philadelphia; settled near Dover, PA.
402. Adam Spohn - Spoghn

576. Thomas Spalding I; born 1640, Suffolk County, England;
     died 1713, St. Mary's County, MD; emigrated about 1658,
     St. Mary's County, MD; married about 1674
577. Catherine Hall
578. Edward Field
580. James Greene I; born Charles County, MD; died 1734,
     Prince George's County, MD; married
581. Charity Hagan; died 1754, Prince George's County, MD
582. Patrick Dyer; born 1680, England; died 1724, Prince
     George's County, MD; married 1702, Prince George's County
583. Comfort Barnes; born 1685, England; died 1760, Prince
     George's County, MD; married second Thomas Edelin
586. Guy Finch; emigrated 1674 from England; died 1688,
     Calvert County, MD; married
587. Rebecca; died about 1712, Prince George's County, MD;
     married second Henry Culver
1152. John Spalding; 1590-1659, Wissett, Suffolk County,
      England
1160. Robert Greene; born 1647, St. Mary's County, MD; died
      about 1707, Charles County, MD; married about 1679
1161. Mary Boarman; born 1660, Boarman's Manor, Charles County,
      MD; died 1716, St. Mary's County, MD
1162. Thomas Hagan; died 1716, Charles County, MD; married
1163. Mary
2304. Augustine Spalding; 1560-1626, Suffolk County, England
2320. Thomas Greene; born about 1610, Bobbing Manor, Kent
      County, England; died 1651, St. Mary's County,MD;
      emigrated 1634, St. Mary's County, MD; married about 1646
2321. Winifred Seybourne; died 1658, St. Mary's County, MD;
      married second Robert Clarke
2322. William Boarman; born about 1625, England; died 1686,
      Boarman's Manor, Charles County, MD; married about 1654
2323. Sarah Linle - Sinley
4608. Thomas Spalding; 1530-1573, of Tynemouth, Suffolk
      County, England
4640. Sir Thomas Greene; died 1624; married
4641. Margaret Webb
9216. John Spalding; 1480-1535, of Tynemouth, Suffolk County,
      England
9280. Robert Greene of Bobbing Manor, Kent County, England;
      married
9281. Frances Darrell
9282. Thomas Webb
18532. John Spalding; 1450-1521, of Farnham, Suffolk County,
       England
18560. Thomas Norton alias Greene
18562. Thomas Darell of Scotney
37120. Sir John Norton of Northwood in Milton, England

"To weave together the fading dates of old manu-
scripts with tradition that has survived sleeping
generations, until the joy and the tears, the quaint
speech and early piety, stand out upon the tapestry
in semblence of a living man, this gives pleasure
which only he who has stood at the loom can feel and
understand." - Essex Antiquarian, Vol. 1, p 150.

In an undertaking such as this there are many who add to the
whole. I wish to acknowledge the assistance of the late Byrle
MacPherson, for the use of her private library known as the
"MacPherson Collection." Also Arthur Cunningham and Harold
Ditzler for their assistance and the use of their private
libraries.

Most information relating to the last generations of these
families has been provided by members of these families. Oral
family history and tradition has been passed down over several
generations, which at times is in error, but for the most part
correct or a basis for further research. Additional research
and documentation has been collected from libraries and
historical societies.

I express my sincere appreciation to the various members of
these families who have assisted in this search.

Leona Cline Bumbaugh, Laura Gilliland Butler, Dora Cline
Carbaugh, Harry and Ada Kump Cline, Evelyn Pittenger Cline,
Elmer Cline, Howard and Jean Kipe Cline, Alan Currens, Harold
Ditzler, Roy and Mary Gilland Eyler, Dorothy Wingate Fitz,
Emory Flohr, Nellie Cline Gilland, John and Emma Bishop Gilland,
Raymond Gilland, Kenneth and Miriam Plank Gilland, Charles and
Lucille West Gilland, Elaine Carbaugh Gilland, Melvin and Rose
Bolland Gilland, Alice Shockey Gilland, Bernard Gilliland, James
Gilliland, Martin and Beulah Gilland Hardman, Mabert Eyler
Harbaugh, Shirley Eyler Hull, Tammie Warren Morris, Emily Willard
Newberry, C.E. Schildknecht, Charles Shindledecker, Earl and
Melva Nagle Shindledecker, Leah L. Spade, Wilbur Stouter, Jessie
Clark Tressler, Samuel Turner, John Turner, Stanley Turner,
Bertha Cline Warren, Stanley Wetzel, Richard Wetzel, Roger and
Cindy Wetzel, Leo Wastler, and Rondie Yancey.

Maryland State Archives, Annapolis, Maryland.
The Historical Society of St. Mary's County, Leonardtown, MD.
The Historical Society of Frederick County, Frederick, Maryland.
The Frederick County Public Libraries, Frederick, Maryland.
The Historical Society of Carroll County, Westminister, Maryland.
The Washington County Free Library, Hagerstown, Maryland.
Mount Saint Mary's College Library, Emmitsburg, Maryland.
The Library of Congress, Washington D.C.
The NSDAR Library, Washington D.C.
The Washington County Historical Society, Hagerstown, Maryland.
The National Archives, Washington D.C.
The Maryland Historical Society, Baltimore, Maryland.
The Historical Society of Adams County, Gettysburg, Pennsylvania.
The Historical Society of York County, York, Pennsylvania.
William Penn Memorial Museum Library, Harrisburg, Pennsylvania.
The Historical Society of Cumberland County, Carlise, PA.
Latter Day Saints Genealogical Library, York, Pennsylvania.
Latter Day Saints Genealogical Library, New Oxford, PA.
The Chester County Historical Society, West Chester, PA.
The Lancaster County Historical Society, Lancaster, PA.
The Mennonite Historical Society, Lancaster, Pennsylvania.
The Historical Society of Pennsylvania, Philadelphia, PA.
Chester County Archives, West Chester, PA.

Baldwin, Jane and Henry, Roberta B., The Maryland Calendar of
    Wills, 1635-1743, Baltimore, Md., 1901-1928.
Barnes, Robert, Maryland Genealogies, A Consolidation of Articles
    from the Maryland Historical Magazine, Vol. I, Genealogical
    Publishing Co., Inc., Baltimore, Md., 1980.
Barnes, Robert, Gleanings from Maryland Newpapers 1727-1775,
    published by Betty Carothers, Lutherville, Md.
Bates, Samuel P., History of Pennsylvania Volunteers 1861-1865,
    B. Singerly, State Printer, Harrisburg, Pa., 1869.
Beitzell, Edwin Warfield, The Jesuit Mission of St. Mary's
    County, Maryland, 1959, no publisher listed, available at
    St. Mary's County Memorial Library, Leonardstown, Md.
Bellis, Geneivieve Hoehn, Our Ancestors, Greens, Wathens, Byrnes,
    Hoehns, and Others, published by Genevieve Hoehn Bellis,
    Arlington, Va., no date.
Bowie, Effie Gwynn, Across the Years in Prince George's County,
    Garrett & Massie, Richmond, Va., 1947.
Brent, Chester Horton, The Descendants of Col. Giles Brent,
    Capt. George Brent, and Robert Brent, Gent., Immigrants to
    Maryland and Virginia, The Tuttle Publishing Co., Rutland,
    Vt., 1946.
Brown, H.W., Prince George's County, Maryland, Indexes of Church
    Registers 1685-1885, Prince George's County Historical
    Society, 1979.
Brugger, Robert J., Maryland, A Middle Temperament 1634-1980,
    John Hopkins University Press, 1988.
Brumbaugh, Gaius Marcus, M.S., Mary Records, Colonial,
    Revolutionary, County, and Church from Original Sources,
    Williams & Wilkins Co., Baltimore, Md., 1915, 1928.
Clements, J.W.S., Origins of Clement - Spalding And Allied
    Families of Maryland and Kentucky, Standard Press,
    Louisville, 1928.
Cooper, William F., The Cooper Family of Maryland, Gateway
    Press, Inc., Baltimore, Md., 1972.
Donnelly, Sister Mary Louise, William Elder, Ancestors and
    Descendants, Published by Sister Mary Louise Donnelly,
    Burke, Va., 1986.
Donnelly, Sister Mary Louise, Maryland Elder Family and Kin,
    William Elder, 1707-1775, Emmitsburg, Maryland, Pioneer,
    Nativity Parish, Burke, Va., 1975.
Donnelly, Sister Mary Louise, Arnold Livers Family In America,
    Mary Loiuse Donnelly, Burke, Va., 1977.
Dorman, John Frederick, Introduction, Genealogy of Virginia
    Families From the Virginia Magazine of History and Biography,
    Genealogical Publishing Co., Inc., Baltimore, Md., 1981.

Eagle, William Henry, M.D., M.A,. Pennsylvania; Genealogies
    chiefly Scotch-Irish and German, Genealogical Publishing
    Company, Inc., Baltimore, Md., 1969.
Eisenberg, Gerson G., Marylanders Who Served The Nation, A
    Biographical Dictionary of Federal Officials from Maryland,
    Maryland State Archives, Annapolis, Md., 1992.
Ellis, Donna M. and Karen A. Stuart, The Calvert Papers,
    Calendar and Guide to the Microfilm Edition, The Maryland
    Historical Society, Baltimore, Md., available at St. Mary's
    County Memorial Library, Leonardtown, Md.
Fenwick, Charles and Leverne, The Spalding Family, a manuscript
    available at St. Mary's County Historical Society, Leonard-
    town, Md.
Forman, Henry Chandler, Jamestown and St. Maries Buried Cities of
    Roamnce, The John Hopkins Press, Baltimore, Md., 1938.
Gilland, Steve, Frederick County, Maryland Backgrounds, Family
    Line Publications, Westminister, Md., 1995.
Gilliland, Mary W. and Oswald P. Gilliland, Our Pioneer Family
    of Gilliland, a booklet available at the Newberry Library,
    Chicago, Ill.
Green, Karen Mauer, The Maryland Gazett 1727-1761, Genealogical
    and Historical Abstracts, The Frontier Press, Galveston, 1989.
Greenham, John, Clans and Families of Ireland, The Heritage
    Press, Wellfleet, Secaucus, New Jersey, 1993.
Greenwood, Mildred Martrue Hutcheson, The Loving Irish - The
    Gillilands, Stephenville Printing Co., Stephenville,
    Tx., 1970.
Hasted, Edward, The History and Topographical Survey of the
    County of Kent, England, by Edward Hasted, of Canterbury,
    Printed by Simmons & Kirkby, Canterbury, 1782.
Hammett, Regina Combs, History of St. Mary's County, Maryland,
    1634-1990, Regina Combs Hammett, Ridge, Md., 1991.
Helman, James A., History of Emmitsburg, Maryland, Citizen Press,
    Frederick, Md., Reprinted 1975 Chronicle Press.
Henry, Mrs. Effie L., Maryland Miscellany, Compiled by Effie
    L. Henry, Washington D.C., Annie Walker Burns, Publisher,
    Washington D.C., 1936.
Hienton, Louise Foyner, Prince George's Heritage, Sidelights on
    the Early History of Prince George's County Maryland from
    1696 to 1800, The Maryland Historical Society, (c) by Louise
    Foyner Hienton.
Holdcraft, Jacob Mehrling, Names In Stone, 75,000 Cemetery
    Inscriptions From Frederick County, Maryland, Ann Arbor, Mi.,
    1966, 2nd printing 1972, distributed by Monocacy Book Co.,
    Redwood City, California.
Irish, Donna R., Pennsylvania German Marriages, Marriages and
    Evidence In Pennsylvania German Churches, Genealogical
    Publishing Co., Inc., Baltimore, Md., 1982.

Jourdan, Elise Greenup, The Land Records of Prince George's
    County, Maryland, 1717 to 1726, Family Line Publications,
    Westminister, Md., 1991.
Jourdan, Elise Greenup, Abstracts of Charles County Maryland
    Court and Land Records, 1658-1665, Family Line Publications,
    Westminister, Md., 1993.
Jourdan, Elise Greenup, Early Families of Southern Maryland,
    Family Line Publications, Westminister, Md., 1992, 1993, 1994.
Kirby, Leta Bricken, Roberts - Wathen And Allied Families, 1970,
    no publisher listed.
Klapthor, Margaret Brown and Paul Dennis Brown, The History of
    Charles County Maryland, Charles County Tercentenary Inc.,
    LaPlata, Md., 1958.
Lake, D.J., 1873 Atlas of Frederick County, Maryland, C.O.
    Titus & Company, Philadelphia, 1873.
Land, Aubrey C., Colonial Maryland, A History, KTO Press,
    Millwood, N.Y., 1981.
Lantz, Emily Emerson, Maryland Heraldry, Baltimore Sun,
    Baltimore, Md., September 9, 1906.
Lynham, C. Richard, The History of A Lynch Family, Descendants
    of John Lynch, Owner of Green's Rest in St. Mary's County,
    Maryland, 1726-1992. A Compilation of Data Subject to Errors,
    Folklore, and Poor Memories, 1993, available at St. Mary's
    County Historical Society, Leonardtown, Md.
MacKenzie, George Norbury, Colonial Families of the United States
    of America, Edited by George Norbury MacKenzie, L.L.B.,
    The Seaforth Press, Genealogical Pubs., Baltimore, Md., 1915.
Magruder, James M., Jr., Index of Maryland Colonial Wills
    1634-1777, In the Hall of Records, Annapolis, Maryland,
    Genealogical Publishing Company, Inc., Baltimore, Md., 1967.
Martin, John Stanwood, Genealogical Index to Frederick County
    Maryland, The First Hundred Years, in four volumes, Conlin's
    Copy Center, Malvern, Pa., 1992.
Matthews, C.M., English Surnames, Weidenfeld and Nicholson,
    London, The Trinity Press, Worcester, London, 1966.
Meline, Mary M. and Rev. Edw. F.X. McSweeny, S.T.D., The Story
    of the Mountain, Mount Saint Mary's College and Seminary,
    Emmitsburg, Maryland, The Weekly Chronicle, Emmitsburg, Md.,
    1911.
Mudd, Richard D., The Mudd Family of the United States, Edwards
    Brothers, Inc., Ann Arbor, Mi., 1951.
Nead, Daniel Wunderlich, The Pennsylvania German Settlement of
    Maryland, Genealogical Publishing Company, Inc., Baltimore,
    Md., 1975.
Newman, Harry Wright, To Maryland From Overseas, Published by
    the Author, Annapolis, Md., 1982, French Bray Co., Glen
    Burnie, Md.

Newman, Harry Wright, The Flowering of the Maryland Palatinate,
    Genealogical Publishing Company, Inc., Baltimore, Md., 1984.
Newman, Harry Wright, Charles County Gentry, Genealogical
    Publishing Company, Inc., Baltimore, Md., 1971.
O'Rourke, Timothy J., Maryland Catholics on the Frontier,
    Brefrey Press, Parsons, Kansas, 1973.
Parran, Alice Norris, Register of Maryland Heraldic Families,
    2 volumes, H.G. Roebuck & Son, Baltimore, Md., 1935, 1938.
Parsons, William Crocker, Ancestry of the Descendants of
    Thomas Attaway Reeder of St. Mary's County, Maryland and a
    Record of the Descendants of Joseph and Elizabeth Spalding
    Parsons, published by the author, Wynnewood, Pa., 1979.
Radoff, M.L., editor, The Old State Line, A History of
    Maryland, Twentieth Century Printing Co., Inc., Baltimore,
    Md., 1971.
Reamy, Martha and Bill Reamy, Immigrant Ancestors of Maryland
    As Found in Local Histories, Waipahu, Hawaii, 1993.
Richardson, Hester Dorsey, Side-Lights on Maryland History
    with Sketches of Early Maryland Families, Genealogical
    Publishing Company, Inc., Baltimore, Md., 1967.
Rutherford, William Kenneth and Anna Clay Zimmerman Rutherford,
    Genealogical History of Our Ancestors, printed in the
    United States of America, 1970.
Scott, Kenneth, Abstracts From Ben Franklin's Pennsylvania
    Gazette, 1728-1748, Genealogical Publishing Company, Inc.,
    Baltimore, Md., 1975.
Scharf, J. Thomas, History of Maryland from the Earliest
    Period to the Present Day, 3 volumes, Tradition Press,
    Hatboro, Pa., 1967.
Schildknecht, C.E., Monocacy and Catoctin, Some Early Settlers
    of Western Maryland and Adjacent Pennsylvania, And Their
    Descendants, 1725-1988, Family Line Publications, Westminister,
    Md., 1989.
Shelton, A. Louise McClinton, Greenwell, Little, Donnally,
    Hardy and Allied Families of Maryland, Kentucky, and
    Missouri, compiled by A. Louise McClinton Shelton,
    Hanford, California.
Shields, John Edgar, A History of the Shields Family, Triangle
    Press, Harrisburg, Pa., 1968.
Skinner, V.L. Jr., Abstracts of the Inventories and Accounts of
    Prerogative Court of Maryland, 1712-1716, Family Line
    Publications, Westminister, Md., 1994.
Skinner, V.L. Jr., Abstracts of the Inventories and Accounts of
    the Prerogative Court of Maryland, 1685-1701, Family Line
    Publications, Westminister, Md., 1992.
Skordas, Gust and Dr. Morris L. Radoff, The Early Settlers of
    Maryland, An Index to Nmaes of Immigrants Compiled From
    Records of Land Patents, 1633-1680 in the Hall of Records,
    Annapolis, Maryland, Genealogical Publishing Company, Inc.,
    Baltimore, Md., 1968.

Smith, Elsdon C., The New Dictionary of American Family Names,
     Harper & Row Publishers, Inc., New York, New York, 1956, 1973.
Spalding, Hughes, The Spalding Family of Maryland, Kentucky,
     And Georgia from 1658 to 1965, The Stein Printing Company,
     Ga., 1963, 1965.
Stein, Charles Francis, A History of Calvert County Maryland,
     The Calvert County Historical Society and Charles Francis
     Stein, Baltimore, Md., 1960.
Tracey, Dr. Grace Louise, Notes From The Records of Old Monocacy,
     by Grace Louise Tracey, Hamstead, Md., 1958, manuscript
     available at the Public Libraries of Frederick County,
     Emmitsburg, Md.
Tracey, Grace L. and John P. Dern, Pioneers of Old Monocacy;
     The Early Settlers of Frederick County, Maryland, 1721 -
     1743, Genealogical Publishing Company, Inc., Baltimore,
     Md., 1987.
Topper, Adele, Alphabetical Roster of Baptisms, Marriages,
     Burials, 'old Church on the Hill, Mt. St. Mary's Catholic
     Church, amanuscript compiled by Adele Topper, Emmitsburg,
     Md., 1982, 1983, available at Mt. St. Mary's College
     Library, Emmitsburg, Md.
Van Horn, R. Lee, Out of the Past, Prince Georgians And Their
     Lands, Prince George's County Historical Society, Riverdale,
     Md., 1976.
Wesley, Irma Hardesty, Hardesty Family In America, no publisher
     listed, Charlotte, N.C., 1981.
Wilcox, Shirley Langdon, C.G., Prince George's County Land
     Records 1696-1702, Prince George's County Genealogical
     Society, Bowie, Md., 1976.
Williams, T.J.C. and Folger McKinsey, History of Frederick
     County Maryland, Titsworth, Frederick, Md., 1910, Baltimore
     Regional Publishing Company, Baltimore, md., 1979.
Wireman, George W., Gateway to the Mountains, Hagerstown
     Bookbinding & Printing Company, Hagerstown, Md., 1969.

INDEX

www.ingramcontent.com/pod-product-compliance
Lightning Source LLC
LaVergne TN
LVHW051700080426
835511LV00017B/2647